Searching Outside The White Box for New Product Innovation

Vision Driving™
*Methods for
Creating Disruptive Product Ideas*

Mark William Zabrowsky

outskirtspress
DENVER, COLORADO

The opinions expressed in this manuscript are solely the opinions of the author and do not represent the opinions or thoughts of the publisher. The author has represented and warranted full ownership and/or legal right to publish all the materials in this book.

Searching Outside The White Box for New Product Innovation
Vision Driving™ Methods for Creating Disruptive Product Ideas
All Rights Reserved.
Copyright © 2015 Mark William Zabrowsky
v4.0

Cover Photo © 2015 Mark William Zabrowsky. All rights reserved - used with permission.

This book may not be reproduced, transmitted, or stored in whole or in part by any means, including graphic, electronic, or mechanical without the express written consent of the publisher except in the case of brief quotations embodied in critical articles and reviews.

Outskirts Press, Inc.
http://www.outskirtspress.com

ISBN: 978-1-4787-5711-5

Outskirts Press and the "OP" logo are trademarks belonging to Outskirts Press, Inc.

PRINTED IN THE UNITED STATES OF AMERICA

Author's Note

As of this printing, *Vision Driving* is a pending Trademark/ Service Mark application for Z-Mark Concepts, Inc.

All other trademarks are the property of their respective companies, or as otherwise noted.

*For my supportive and loving family and friends:
Judy, Phil, Jennifer, Bonnie, Ellen, Steve,
Mort, Jim, Liza, and Marcie.*

Introduction

I have spent the bulk of my career in developing new consumer products and have seen a multitude of company approaches in the new product development (NPD) function. From my personal experiences as well as observations of the business world, it is clear to me that most companies want innovation, but many are not satisfied with their own results.

Why is this?

NPD is a vital and integral part of the future health, profitability, and market value of companies. Without a successful NPD function there is the chance that a company will become marginalized within their industry. There are too many examples of companies that suffered great losses because their NPD function could not keep pace with the changing world. Such companies as Kodak, Nokia, and Blockbuster, were all marginalized by others who pursued the more disruptive NPD opportunities.

Companies can have different reasons to seek a viable NPD function:

1. Deliver incremental revenue growth each year beyond their organic growth.

2. Proactively help maintain or improve their competitive advantage and share position in their current marketplace.

3. Reactively defend their position with a new product launch as a response to a competitive entry.

4. Revitalize and recycle a mature or declining business into a high growth business.

5. Extend their presence into markets new to the company.

6. Create a new-to-the-world segment, or sub-segment.

For those companies which operate in markets with short product life cycles, the necessity for a healthy NPD function is a matter of life or death. If they do not bring innovations to the market, they will be quickly overrun by their competition. Several different classes of goods come to mind as examples: room air fresheners, running shoes, skin renewal, diet aids, and today's Smartphone war.

For many companies, the NPD results are often not steady. Some good years are followed by bad years, and some launch successes are followed by launch failures. Although the exact number is indeterminate because of the different criteria used, it is generally accepted that more than half of all new consumer products fail to achieve their performance objectives in the marketplace.

Most companies want to improve their stats on performance but are unable to find the sweet spot approach that is right for them. Many, but clearly not all companies today, follow a best practices approach for the new product development process. The most mentioned of these is The Stage-Gate® process (a registered trademark of the Product Development Institute Inc.) as developed by Dr. Robert G. Cooper. This method defines the steps for taking NPD ideas through a screening and vetting process from idea formation at the front end of the idea funnel, through idea screening, product development, and finally, commercialization. Some believe that if they get the process right, then they will have a successful new products program. While a good process is important, it is not a guarantor of commercial success. There are other factors that contribute to a successful NPD function. The greatest likelihood of success comes when all factors are optimized.

While some companies do have it just right, many do not. Worse, there are many companies that don't know what is wrong, or how to fix it. This has always frustrated me as I look at the dozens of business books and case studies written on the subject. Certainly some of these have merit and could help if applied within the company.

There are probably as many reasons for poor NPD performance as there are outside consultants who are brought in and paid handsomely to answer that question. My general belief is that unsatisfactory results stem from a short list:

1. The NPD function is headed by the wrong person, without a proper mix of marketing and product development skill sets, NPD experience, imagination, vision, and leadership abilities.

2. Not having the right balance to the NPD function between structure and discipline, and sound judgment and flexibility. The optimal process needs both.

3. Lack of an innovation culture, without an inspired, challenged, motivated, and empowered company staff.

4. Poor execution of the launch.

5. Poor management of the front end funnel of ideas resulting in too few ideas generated and/or ideas with a low degree of innovation. Either way, this leaves the company with fewer good ideas to pursue, and creates the pressure to pursue less

than optimal ideas through launch. The NPD process is one of attrition. Without a healthy volume of good ideas at the front end, there is a tendency to lower the screening hurdles in the vetting process and become married to the wrong ideas, for lack of any better alternatives. Wrong decisions are made and wrong ideas are pursued.

There are many books written about the causes for the high rate of NPD failures. This is not one of them. There are also many books written about the NPD process in screening, developing, and launching new products. This book is not one of them either.

This book focuses on the 5th issue in the above list, not by dwelling on a deep analysis, but rather by offering a method for generating more new product ideas, and better ideas, with a higher level of innovation. By improving both the quantity and quality of NPD ideas at the front end of the NPD funnel, the individual or company will have a better chance in ultimately launching good ideas and the right ideas.

In this book I talk about generating not just more innovative ideas, but more disruptive innovative ideas. So, what are disruptive new products? Why is disruptive NPD so desirable? Why and when should we seek them?

Within the spectrum of NPD products, there is a range of innovation from low level linear changes, to low level innovations, to higher level disruptive innovations that change paradigms within a segment, and sometimes well beyond the segment. The latter are often referred to as high level disruptive innovations. Historical examples of paradigm changing disruptive innovations with far reaching effects would include Gutenberg's printing press, the telescope, telephone, the electric light bulb, personal computers and the internet. Lower level disruptions, where the effect is limited to within the segment or has the effect of creating a new sub-segment, might include florescent light bulbs, Transitions® focal lenses, power steering and automatic transmissions in cars, fabric softeners, the first electric blanket, no-frost refrigerators, the first electric pencil sharpeners, and Breath Right® nasal strips.

The size of the prize, a term that is often used these days, is in some way related to the level of innovation of an NPD entry. It is therefore reasonable to understand why companies would like to pursue more disruptive innovation for the bigger prize.

This book describes specific scenarios where a company should consider pursuing disruptive NPD ideas as part of its overall competitive strategies. In some cases disruptive NPD can be viewed as appropriate and even necessary to support specific company objectives.

1. Seeking meaningful revenue growth.

2. Maintaining dominance within a segment.

3. Seeking dramatic share gain in an existing arena.

4. Recycling a mature or declining segment to create and own a new embryonic high growth sub-segment.

5. Entering a market new for the company.

6. Creating a new-to-the-world segment, or sub-segment.

7. Defending against a competitive disruptive entry.

Seeking any level of innovation is a difficult undertaking. Seeking disruptive innovation is a far more challenging task. In this book I first expose the limitations of current NPD best practices in generating disruptive NPD ideas, and then I offer a step by step approach for advancing on those practices to generate a range of new disruptive NPD ideas.

The starting point in the current best practice approach for generating NPD ideas often relies on consumer research to unearth unfulfilled consumer needs, or need-gaps, often called the White Space, or as I call it, the White Box. The next step is to develop new product ideas that address and fulfill these unfulfilled consumer needs. I have seen countless examples where the *exclusive* reliance on this approach has led to lackluster NPD ideas. Why? Because the consumer's vision of what they want, and what they ask for, is limited by their own experiences. The consumer need-gap insight, with its inherent limitations, becomes a handicap to what the marketer then goes on to pursue as a new product idea.

Disruptive ideas don't come from this type of consumer research. They come from the inspiration of the ideators. What is needed, and what is offered in this book, is thinking that goes beyond the White Box for a search of higher quality new disruptive ideas. In our time Steve Jobs has said it best, as captured in one of his most often referenced quote: *"It's really hard to design products by focus groups. A lot of times, people don't know what they want until you show it to them."* And as we all have witnessed, Steve Jobs has also done it best.

So how is it done? How do we go beyond the obvious need-gaps of consumer research? How can we improve our NPD performance in developing a robust range of disruptive NPD ideas at the front end of the innovation funnel?

In this book I present a mental journey I call Vision Driving™, a method for generating new disruptive NPD ideas....by Searching Outside The White Box. The method is based first on observations of historical examples of innovations, which are deconstructed to reveal their possible ideation processes. From this we begin to see how certain mental stimuli have, and can be used, to create that moment of eureka for a disruptive idea. These stimuli become the foundation for the Vision Driving process. But there is more to it.

With references to other perspectives and thinking methods such as Brainstorming, Synectics, The Scientific Method, *The Innovator's Dilemma, The Butterfly Effect,* Trending Analysis, Challenging Beliefs, and others, I have been able to construct this prescribed process to Vision Driving. It is a journey of creative thinking and idea building that yields new ideas, some feasible today, others as only a vision.

Vision Driving creates disruption, so don't look for new ideas that are merely linear extensions of the existing. Just as many innovations in science have their roots in science fiction before they became science fact, Vision Driving may produce ideas that seem like marketing fiction today and act as the inspiration for the birthing of new marketing fact. This is the key to Vision Driving. It forces us to look well beyond the obvious to conjure up what might seem like the absurd today. Like in ice hockey where you skate to where the puck will be, Vision Driving takes the ideator to where the opportunities will be.

This book provides descriptions and rationale for the 8 progressive Vision Driving steps from the first step of *Defining the Business* to the last step of *Idea Formation*. It provides guidance for practicing Vision Driving by the individual or within a company group setting, and offers a visual mapping tool which helps stimulate the mental progression in the Vision Driving process.

The process provides a multitude of benefits in the search for NPD ideas:

1. It is designed to stretch our imagination in generating disruptive NPD ideas.

2. It is capable of stimulating a range of ideas to satisfy the need for a healthy volume of NPD ideas at the front end of the NPD Stage-Gate process.

3. The developed NPD ideas can create the descriptions of new technology and/or technology applications, *before the consumers ask for it.*

4. The NPD ideas with their new technology or technology applications can become the basis for motivating the actual creation of the new technology that may not yet exist.

5. The NPD ideas may offer the business incentive for identifying derivative ideas that use more viable, do-able today technology, while still maintaining sufficient appeal and revenue potential.

In the later chapters I help jump start your developing Vision Driving skills by demonstrating how Vision Driving can be used to create a range of disruptive NPD ideas within specific business arenas, as in these examples:

- **Sun intensity monitor and alert** in the form of a wearable patch, headband, wristband, or on the brim of a hat, or as a tiny dot imbedded in sunglasses that changes color when the sun's intensity and duration reach a dangerous limit.

- **Foot self-massaging shoes** that can be activated on demand when someone is sitting while resting their feet, in their shoes, up on a ledge or stool.

- **A sound cancellation or deflection appliance that sits in a room** and creates a sound resistant force field like an invisible sound deflection umbrella, to prevent or reduce unwanted sound from entering a room.

- **Germ detection surface wipes, and / or allergens detection wipes** that change different colors wherever they are wiped on a surface and make contact with bacteria, viruses, or allergens.

- **In-home food sterilization appliance,** that sits on a countertop and provides the consumer with their own means to control food safety.

Vision Driving can be viewed as one integral step of a strategic pathway for achieving specific company objectives. If the objective is to disrupt a company's linear trajectory for revenue and / or market position, then a disruptive NPD launch may be necessary, and Vision Driving will help formulate a funnel of new disruptive NPD ideas.

There are many ways to be creative and inspired. There are many ways that innovations have been created and will be created. There will never be just one method for creating disruptive NPD ideas. Vision Driving adds a new perspective to the contemporary best practices approaches to NPD ideation. The very nature of the process is designed to go beyond linear creative thinking to drive disruption.

Throughout my career I have been applying bits and pieces of what I now call the Vision Driving process to my work as a marketer and ideator. Along the way I have developed a range of new products using these techniques, while at the same time building and refining this process. It is a valuable guide that can be put into practice by any solo individual or company, from small businesses to Fortune 500 companies, from junior marketing executives to CEOs, which have the courage to get out in front of the competitive change curve within their business arena.

I fully expect and believe that the more Vision Driving is used to create disruptive NPD ideas, the more it can be further refined and improved upon. Enjoy the read, develop your own Vision Driving skills, and let me hear your comments and inputs.

Mark William Zabrowsky
Zmarkconceptsinc@gmail.com

Contents

Chapter 1: The Role of Disruptive New Products in a
Competitive Strategy 1
Chapter 2: The Funnel vs The Straw 29
Chapter 3: What is the White Box ? 34
Chapter 4: White Box Limitations 39
Chapter 5: The Vision Driving Process - Searching in the
Expansion Space 48
Chapter 6: Vision Driving Essentials 70
Chapter 7: Defining the Business 80
Chapter 8: Immersion in the Arena 92
Chapter 9: Trending Analysis - Observation Tools 94
Chapter 10: Trending Analysis - Application Tools 113
Chapter 11: Challenging Beliefs 128
Chapter 12: Borrowing and / or Combining Behavior 132
Chapter 13: Borrowing and / or Combining Technology 137
Chapter 14: Mind Tools That Stimulate Imagination 142
Chapter 15: Vision Driving and Idea Mapping in a
Company Setting 145
Chapter 16: Vision Driving Applications 164
Chapter 17: Vision Driving Applications - Foot Products 167
Chapter 18: Vision Driving Applications - Sun Protection 178
Chapter 19: Vision Driving Applications – Home Interior
Air/Ambiance Conditioning 186
Chapter 20: Vision Driving Applications – Value Added Wipes ... 193
Chapter 21: Vision Driving Applications - Food Storage &
Protection 204
Summary 210
About the Author 212

CHAPTER 1

The Role of Disruptive New Products in a Competitive Strategy

As stated in the title, this book offers search methods for creating disruptive new product ideas. Before delving into the process, it makes sense to understand the meaning of disruption, its merits, and why and when we should consider it in helping us achieve our business goals and objectives.

In the dictionary, the word disrupt is defined by the act of breaking apart or throwing something into disorder. That doesn't sound like something we want. But when viewed in the world of economic activity and marketing, disruption is a fact of life, whether we want it or not, and whether it produces good or bad effects. Disruption in the supply of copper, or disruption in train service can each have unfavorable consequences to the status quo, while disruption caused by the replacement of cash transactions with charge cards, or the disruption caused by motorized vehicles replacing horses, or the invention of the telephone, all had mostly favorable effects.

Disruption can take place in any of the dimensions of a business. It can manifest itself in a new-to-the-world product or service, or the way a product is configured or the way needs are satisfied and the

SEARCHING OUTSIDE THE WHITE BOX FOR NEW PRODUCT INNOVATION

benefits delivered. But disruption can also occur in the way products are manufactured, or in the way products and services are distributed or delivered. Amazon® demonstrated the latter type of disruption by changing the dynamics of retailing by redefining how products were "delivered" to the consumer. Disruption changes the winners and losers in a business segment. While the disruptor can become the winner, those who are disrupted out, may become the losers.

In the world of product innovation and NPD, disruption is a good thing. It is the term applied to new product entries that change the paradigm of needs and behavior, and typically reap big rewards to the disruptor in sales, share, and profits. Disruptive new products provide new, better ways to satisfy needs, and in many cases satisfies needs that weren't even articulated. And, there are some disruptive innovations that have far reaching effects well beyond the business segment.

Disruptive NPD is just one type of innovation strategy. At the lower end of the NPD innovation spectrum there are the linear innovation updates, sometimes as product renovations, and sometimes as line extensions, like changes in size, feature upgrades, added benefits, packaging, form, color, flavor, etc. The objectives might include:

A. Keeping the product, brand, or service updated, relevant, and appealing to the consumer.

B. Maintaining competitive share position.

C. Seeking competitive advantage and / or share growth. In cases where the competition does not respond in kind, the first to market such renovations or line extensions may enjoy some share growth.

D. Growing revenue via product upgrades and / or line extensions.

E. Maintaining Trade interest and distribution.

THE ROLE OF DISRUPTIVE NEW PRODUCTS IN A COMPETITIVE STRATEGY

Hence, for both offensive and defensive reasons, the number one task of all marketers is to maintain the viability of the business through such linear innovations. Some examples of these include:

- Mr. Clean® household cleansers adding Febreze® odor neutralizing fragrances.

- Car motor oil brands that added new integral pouring spout packaging.

- Apple®'s next generation iPhone ® 6 Smart Phone.

- Facial tissues with added skin moisturizers and aloe.

- Coffee makers with auto-off features.

- Maximum strength OTC Drug products.

- Initial entries of Pepto-Bismol® tablets and capsule forms.

- The first combination of toothpaste plus whitening.

- Longer life light bulbs.

- Battery packaging with built in battery strength tester.

- Tylenol®' s continual line extensions with new extra strength and extended relief analgesic formulas, new benefits (beyond basic analgesic pain and fever relief), new forms such as capsules, and line extensions into children's remedies.

Then there are disruptive innovations which themselves come in degrees. At the lower end of disruptive innovations are those that have

SEARCHING OUTSIDE THE WHITE BOX FOR NEW PRODUCT INNOVATION

a profound impact but usually limited to within the new or existing business segment itself. These disruptors can:

A. Spark a dramatic renewal of sales growth within an existing business segment, or the creation of new sources of revenue from a newly created sub-segment.

B. Typically provide the marketer with the benefits of premium pricing and increased profit margins.

C. Create a new-to-the world segment

D. Change consumer attitudes and behavior.

E. Generate increased appeal, acceptance, and growth in the user base or the creation of new users.

F. Render an existing product or method obsolete.

Such examples include:

- Introduction of Febreze® odor elimination sprays, as a new sub-segment in household air freshening.

- The creation of a new sub-segment in OTC Drug cold care with a new benefit of cold duration reduction, with such products as Cold- EEZE® Cold remedy lozenges, and Zicam® Pre-Cold® remedy.

- Power steering and automatic transmissions in cars.

- Apple®'s first launch of the iPhone®, creating the first Smartphone.

THE ROLE OF DISRUPTIVE NEW PRODUCTS IN A COMPETITIVE STRATEGY

- Apple®'s first launch of the iPad® as a new segment in hand held information devices.

- Transitions® focal lenses, which created a new type of value added segment in eyeglasses, and replacing the awkward behavior of carrying separate eyewear for indoor vs. outdoor usage.

- The initial introduction of the Black & Decker ® Dustbuster ®, the first hand held portable vacuum cleaner.

- Fluorescent light bulbs created a new sub-segment in lighting that provided better lighting, energy efficiency, and new usage applications.

- The first liquid laundry fabric softeners for consumer use, considered as either a new sub-segment in laundry care or a new-to-the-world segment of fabric conditioners.

- OTC Whitening strips brought consumers a new way of whitening teeth at home, and established a new sub-segment in oral care.

- Breathe Right® nasal strips were a new sub-segment in nasal congestion relief.

- P&G's launch of the first disposable diapers as a new-to-the-world segment basically rendering reusable cloth diapers obsolete.

- Post it® notes created a new sub-segment in office supplies.

- The OTC availability of cryogenic wart removers (previously provided exclusively within doctor's offices) offered a new and more effective OTC method for consumers to remove warts vs. the established OTC Drug liquid applicators. This change created a new OTC sub-segment in wart removal, at a higher premium price and profitability, and replaced many doctor office visits for such treatment.

- The first electric blanket created a new sub-segment in bedding by bringing the heating feature of electricity to bedding, allowing consumers greater control over their comfort, with the added advantage of reducing their household heating costs.

- No-frost refrigerators were a huge advancement in home food storage that eliminated the inconvenience of periodic manual defrosting. This new feature drove consumers to abandon their current refrigerator (probably before its lifespan was over) and buy a new refrigerator. This is a perfect example of the strategic value of disruptive innovation in making an existing product obsolete.

At the highest end of the disruption spectrum are the game changers that offer new-to-the-world solutions. Those innovations are the high disruptors that have broad impact inside and beyond a segment, which can include:

A. New-to-the-world ways of doing things, seeing things, understanding things, with a dramatic shift in consumer attitudes and behavior.

B. Creation of new segments with an entirely new set of users.

C. Dramatic macro effects well beyond the segment, possibly affecting all types of human activities, including economic, industrial, societal, geo-political, religious, health, and so forth.

D. Rendering an existing product or method obsolete.

THE ROLE OF DISRUPTIVE NEW PRODUCTS IN A COMPETITIVE STRATEGY

E. If a commercial activity, it could create rapid increases in sales and share, virtually all incremental, while at the same time providing the benefits of premium pricing and increased profit margins.

Some of these advancements include:

- The first needle-and-thread allowed man to create garments from animal skins allowing him to migrate and survive in colder climates.

- Gutenberg's printing press brought education to the masses, which then helped accelerate the Renaissance.

- The steam engine dramatically improved man's ability to perform work beyond his own manual strength. It helped spark the industrial revolution and move man from an agrarian society to industrial, which in turn changed the makeup of society itself.

- The invention of firearms helped alter the eco-social-political landscape of societies and helped contribute to the erosion of the feudal system. Firearms helped redistribute power from the wealthy elite upper class who could afford body armor, to the peasants who could now afford weaponry to challenge the rulers.

- The telescope was literally a world changing innovation. It changed man's view of his place in the universe, and drove disruption in the Church's hold on power, knowledge, and influence in Europe, and ultimately gave way to the Renaissance.

- The telephone was a lot more than a new form of communication. It accelerated man's advancements in every form of human social and economic activity.

SEARCHING OUTSIDE THE WHITE BOX FOR NEW PRODUCT INNOVATION

- The electric light bulb turned night into day, increased mankind's productive hours, and changed the economic and social dynamics of work, play, relationships, and more.

- Personal computers and the internet affected all manner of human interaction and productivity. It changed the dynamics of work, the nature of communications, and continues to have a dramatic effect on social interactions. In a way, this innovation was the second coming of Gutenberg's printing press in how it expanded the reach of communications and knowledge for all mankind.

- Oral contraceptives were not just a new form of birth control. This innovation gave women the control over their bodies and helped accelerate their sexual, social, and economic freedom.

So, given this range, how should a company choose which type of innovation strategy to pursue? Where and when does disruptive NPD fit within their competitive strategies? And what degree of disruption makes most sense?

In answering these questions, we need to recognize that NPD strategies of any type should align with and support a company's overall strategies. As stated in the introduction, companies seek an NPD function for one or more reasons:

1. Deliver incremental revenue growth each year beyond their organic growth.

2. Proactively help maintain or improve their competitive advantage and share position in their current marketplace.

THE ROLE OF DISRUPTIVE NEW PRODUCTS IN A COMPETITIVE STRATEGY

3. Reactively defend their position with a new product launch as a response to a competitive entry.

4. Revitalize and recycle a mature or declining business into a high growth business.

5. Extend their presence into markets new to the company.

6. Create a new-to-the-world segment, or sub-segment.

That's pretty much a generic starting point in defining an NPD strategy. But what specific NPD strategies are best for a company, and best for its individual operating segments?

Before a company can determine their optimal role and type of NPD strategies, they must first formulate their overall company goals and strategic objectives. How they do this is quite varied as there are multiple strategic planning methods. In my view, one of the most productive methods is at least based in part on the work by Michael E. Porter. In his great book *Competitve Strategy* he postulates that an extensive review of internal and external factors will guide the company towards what he refers to as an appropriate set of strategies to consider. He uses this term, *appropriate*, to define a template of strategies that offer the greatest likelihood for success. He maintains that pursuit of any other strategies for that particular company will present greater challenges, requiring greater resources, and yet still have lesser chances for success.

Following Porter's approach to strategic planning, some of the factors that might be studied include the following:

- Company's mission statement.

- Company's overall growth objectives.

- Its internal strengths, competitive strengths and weaknesses, resources, assets.

- Competitive landscape, i.e. is it concentrated in the hands of one or two marketers or is it fragmented among many?

- The company's position within a business segment, i.e. is the company or brand the dominant player, or one of several dominant players, or one of several groups of players?

- Is their current position strong, favorable, weak, or untenable?

- What is the basis of competition within the segment?

- Barriers to entry.

- Pricing trends, and whether it enjoys price leadership or is it a price follower.

- Role of forward and backward integration.

- Competitive requisites within the business arena, such as access to materials and supplies, technology, high speed manufacturing, production capacity, human resources, etc.

- Regulatory environment.

- Segment life cycle.

When they are all considered, these factors will help determine the appropriate competitive strategies that offer the greatest likelihood for success for that particular company and within each of its business segments. This becomes Porter's template for appropriate strategies. When done correctly, this template will guide the company in

THE ROLE OF DISRUPTIVE NEW PRODUCTS IN A COMPETITIVE STRATEGY

making the optimal strategic decisions for each of its operating segments, such as:

- Should the company or brand maintain its current share position and draw profits?

- Should it maintain or change its competitive strategy of differentiation, low cost, or niche player?

- Should it pursue a different positioning strategy within the business arena where it many benefit from a stronger competitive position?

- Pursue aggressive share gaining initiatives?

- Re-energize or re-cycle a mature business?

- Expand distribution in current markets?

- Create entirely new segments?

- Enter existing markets new to the company?

- Strengthen internal skills and resources, manufacturing capacity, and / or access to resources?

- Pursue aggressive cost containment?

- Execute pricing actions?

- Increase vertical integration?

- Seek strategic acquisitions, mergers, and partnerships?

- Exit a segment, or abandon some form of integration?

SEARCHING OUTSIDE THE WHITE BOX FOR NEW PRODUCT INNOVATION

Once it is set, the overall strategic plan provides the foundation for the selection of the appropriate NPD strategies to support the strategic plans within each of its operating segments:

- Should the company cease all support for the particular business, including NPD, and draw profits that could be used to fund other company endeavors?

- Should the company pursue a modest program of product renovations and linear line extensions?

- Where should the company pursue more aggressive NPD programs, and at what level of innovation?

- Which of its operating segments within its portfolio should be given high priority for NPD, and which should be given lower priority?

- Where is NPD seen as a defensive strategy and where is it seen as offensive?

- Should the company use NPD to create new-to-the-world segments, or new sub-segments, or expand into existing markets new to the company, and which type of NPD is necessary?

- What resources would be required, and which ones can be brought to bear?

Among the many factors in the strategic planning process that help determine the template of appropriate NPD strategies, there are two that stand out: 1) the company's brand share position within the landscape of the arena, and 2) the life cycle of that arena. An understanding of these factors will help contribute to the larger determination of which

THE ROLE OF DISRUPTIVE NEW PRODUCTS IN A COMPETITIVE STRATEGY

type of NPD initiatives to pursue, and where disruptive NPD is appropriate and possibly even necessary.

First, regarding **share position** within the competitive arena, there are several scenarios that can help shape NPD strategies:

1. If the company is in **a dominant share position**, it behooves the company to remain dominant, and to do so it must innovate. If they don't, it is only a question of time before another brand will challenge them for that position. The risk for any dominant brand is an assault on their position at any time and by any marketer, whether currently a player in the business segment or not. For this reason, a dominant brand should always seek to innovate to maintain its position. The type of innovations that a leader pursues depends on their strategic objectives, their resources, their level of risk tolerance, and as detailed below, the life cycle of the segment. If the objective is to maintain their competitive advantage and share position, then lower level innovations such as line extensions or renovations may be adequate. But this approach has inherent risks. If the competition acts more aggressively, then the dominant brand is immediately confronted with a scramble to find defensive follow ups. In the case of a dominant brand within a mature or declining segment, it should be the leader, more so than any of its competitors, to re-energize the segment via a disruptive new product launch. This company has the resources and the benefit of its inertial position with the consumer and trade to launch such innovations and be accepted. Leaders are expected to lead, and expected to innovate to stay as leaders. If not, others will fill the vacuum now or later. When choosing to execute a disruptive NPD launch, a dominant brand can strengthen its position within an existing segment, or extend its position into a newly created sub-segment. Some examples:

◄ SEARCHING OUTSIDE THE WHITE BOX FOR NEW PRODUCT INNOVATION

- P&G® was already in a dominant position in household cleaning when it launched Swiffer®, creating a new sub-segment in household cleaning devices.

- Crest® Whitestrips® created a new sub-segment in OTC oral care, with a new source of revenue.

- Apple®'s first launch of the iPad® was a new sub-segment in hand held electronic information devices.

- Best Buy®, a key player within the bricks and mortar electronics retailers, launched the Geek Squad® tech support service as a new sub-segment within this class of retailers.

- Dr. Scholl's®, a dominant player in foot care, extended their presence in retail accounts with the creation of in-store self-serve kiosks offering customized orthotic shoe inserts.

- McDonald's® was already a leader in fast food restaurants when it introduced the idea of fast breakfast food starting in 1972. This was a huge success and source of meaningful growth for the chain. By 1987, 25% of all breakfasts eaten out of the home were from McDonalds.

- Gillette®'s most recent advancement in shavers, Fusion® Proglide® Power Razor with Flexball ™ Technology, provides a closer, more comfortable shave with a razor that rolls along the contours of the face.

- Kimberly Clark® was already a dominant player in paper goods when it helped create the new segment of adult incontinence products with its launch of Depend® brand of incontinence products.

THE ROLE OF DISRUPTIVE NEW PRODUCTS IN A COMPETITIVE STRATEGY

- Nike® is one of the most innovative companies, demonstrating a range of strategic moves that have maintained and extended its dominance in athletic wear and accessories. First establishing itself as a dominant player in athletic footwear by building disruption into their products, such as Nike Air® athletic shoes, the company has since continually redefined its business, extending into new sub-segments, again with disruptive NPD entries. Nike is a model for successful dominant companies that have used disruption as a fundamental tool in making on-going strategic moves.

2. In the case where a company has **no share presence within an existing segment and wishes to enter**, then executing a disruptive NPD launch is not only appropriate but necessary. Unless the company is considering an entry as the value price brand or low cost supplier, it is essential that the company enter the segment with a product or service that offers new and better ways to meet consumer needs via a disruptive entry. Without some type of disruption, a new entry into an existing segment will be fighting an uphill battle for share with the existing players who will be defending their turf. And if the goal is to create a new-to-the-world segment, then disruption is mandatory. Whether we call it a new sub-segment or new-to-the-world segment is a semantically moot point. The need for disruption is the same. Some examples where a non-player created a new sub-segment or a new-to-the-world segment might include:

- Both Zicam® and Cold EEZE® were new to the cold segment when launched.

- The initial launch of Dustbuster® by Black & Decker®.

SEARCHING OUTSIDE THE WHITE BOX FOR NEW PRODUCT INNOVATION

- The Beano® brand had no position in OTC digestive aids when it launched the first gas prevention product, creating a new sub-segment.

- Tesla® created the high-end electric car segment.

- Red Bull® and 5-Hour Energy® were non-players in energy drinks when launched.

- Method® created a new segment in household cleaners with more attractive, elegant, and ergonomic packaging.

- Sanka® coffee was one of the earliest brands of decaffeinated coffee, creating a very strong sub-segment in the hot beverage arena, and soon became synonymous with "the alternative coffee for close to bedtime".

- Breathe Right® nasal strips created a new segment in nose congestion relief by inventing a physical method (spring flex external applicator) vs. the OTC Drug nasal sprays.

- Apple®'s first launch of the iPhone®.

- Panasonic® electric pencil sharpener.

- P&G®'s launch of the first disposable diapers.

- OXO® kitchen food preparation tools with emphasis on ergonomics and style.

- GoPro® action cameras created a new sub-segment in photography for personalized hands free video self-recording of action events.

THE ROLE OF DISRUPTIVE NEW PRODUCTS IN A COMPETITIVE STRATEGY

3. **For a company or brand with any share position witnessing the launch by a new competitive disruptive product entry into their arena,** an NPD response would be necessary to defend their position. If the response is a me-too product then we really can't call the fast follower a disruptor, but the response may be adequate to maintain its position. But, if the defending company responds with its own next generation innovation, then we may see another disruption in the segment, putting the competition at risk. Some examples of fast followers with similar or better innovations:

- Schick® and Bic® have for years been fast followers of Gillette® within the disposable razor blade business, often following the innovations of the leader with their own me-too shavers.

- All those car manufacturers which launched their own versions of electric cars or hybrids in response to the Toyota® Prius® which was the first mass produced hybrid vehicle.

- Amazon® launched the Kindle® electronic reader, and Barnes & Nobles® launched their NOOK® reader in response to the Apple® iPad®.

- Many established soup marketers launched their own versions of heat and serve cups of soups in response to the 1970's disruptive entry by Top Ramen® cup of noodles soup, which established a new sub-segment in store bought soup preparations.

- Virtually all retail banks followed the lead of Chemical Bank when they opened the first full featured US ATM in 1969 in Rockville Center, New York.

- Following the successful entry of the iPhone® from Apple®, the first smart cell phone, other electronics manufacturers quickly joined in.

4. **In all other share position scenarios within a crowded field of many players,** the type of NPD strategies that a company or brand chooses to pursue depends on the strategic objectives. If based on the strategic planning process a company has decided that share maintenance is appropriate, and accepts the risk of more aggressive competitive moves, then low level NPD initiatives like renovations and/or line extensions might make sense. In such a crowded field, any company can theoretically execute a disruptive entry to gain competitive advantage. This scenario is one of the most interesting in the world of marketing, and whenever there is a disruption it causes excitement in the segment for the company, the consumer, and the Trade. It also causes consternation for the remaining companies which must respond in kind or lose some position. Some examples:

   - Bayer®, a brand among many in OTC Drug internal analgesics, introduced Aleve®, the first all day relief internal analgesic, and extended its overall share within OTC Drug internal analgesics.

   - Toyota® gained market share position with its launch of the Prius®, which was the first mass produced hybrid vehicle.

   - The Vicks® brand was competing among many players in the cold care segment when it introduced NyQuil® liquid cold relief products in the mid 1960's. Until then the liquid treatments were predominantly for cough relief. NyQuil was not only a new form, but was one of the first

THE ROLE OF DISRUPTIVE NEW PRODUCTS IN A COMPETITIVE STRATEGY

liquid cold remedies to focus on relieving the particular discomforts of night time cold sufferers.

- When Chemical Bank introduced the first full featured US ATM in 1969 it was one of many retail banks competing for New York customers. Although there were other attempts at this new form of banking, it was Chemical Bank that installed a new machine, called the Docuteller, which for the first time, made use of a reusable, magnetically coded card to withdraw cash. This caused a real disruption in the industry as it changed the paradigm of retail banking service availability, a change which continues to this day. Although Chemical Bank did not maintain any exclusivity to this new service, it did benefit from being the first.

- With the increasing appeal and usage of portable electronic devices, the need for longer lasting batteries has become a race among many players. In the early 1990's Sony® Corporation was the first to introduce the rechargeable lithium-ion battery which had some special advantages over the existing choice for mobile power, the nickel-cadmium battery. A key feature of Sony's new battery was its higher energy density, twice that of the nickel-cadmium type, which meant that a smaller size battery could provide more power. This had a significant disruptive effect on the portable electronics segment allowing for smaller and lighter devices. Sony quickly gained share in supplying the growing mobile device market, but as others joined in, and with their own advances, Sony could not maintain any real exclusivity.

- Transitions Optical was one of many manufacturers of optical lenses for eyewear. Then in the early 1990's they were the first to market a photochromic lens that changes colors in the exposure to sunlight. This was a new sub-segment in eyewear, offering very appealing benefits to consumers, and providing the company with a premium priced line, and significant source of revenue growth. Their Transitions® lenses are now the #1 recommended brand, with several competitors following their lead.

- By the 1950's televisions were becoming part of the American household, and there were nearly a dozen brands competing for this growing market, including such names as RCA®, Dumont®, Philco®, GE®, Westinghouse®, Zenith®, and others. The use of wireless remote controls was gaining ground in a few consumer electronics products, but had not yet been applied to televisions. Zenith was the first brand to take the lead by offering a full service TV remote controller in the mid 1950's, and for this innovation, they enjoyed early acceptance and growth. Other brands followed suit as consumers recognized the importance of this convenience. The TV paradigm was forever changed, and we saw the early emergence of the couch potato. Unfortunately for Zenith, they were not able to keep pace with the required high rate of innovations to stay competitive within the TV arena.

In summary regarding **share position**, our focus in this book is on those share position scenarios where a disruptive NPD strategic move is appropriate, and possibly necessary:

- To maintain our dominant share position in a segment.

- Enter into a segment new to us where we have no share.

- Secure meaningful share gain within one of our operation segments.

- Extend our share position via creation of a new sub-segment.

THE ROLE OF DISRUPTIVE NEW PRODUCTS IN A COMPETITIVE STRATEGY

- Defend our share position in response to a competitive disruptive NPD entry.

The second factor that stands out in the overall strategic planning function, and especially as in regard to NPD planning, is the notion of **segment life cycle**. The segment life cycle reveals insights that will shape a strategy for NPD in general and disruptive NPD in particular. The segment's life cycle will tell us where disruption is taking place and where it is not, and where it could best be pursued for greatest rewards.

In the early stages of a life cycle, disruption is already occurring and demonstrating its effect on the world with rapid acceptance, growth, and profit generation. In the mature and declining stages of the life cycle, there is little or no disruption occurring. In those stages, the segment has saturated its potential, profits are being squeezed, and the name of the game is brand differentiation, cost containment, and share maintenance.

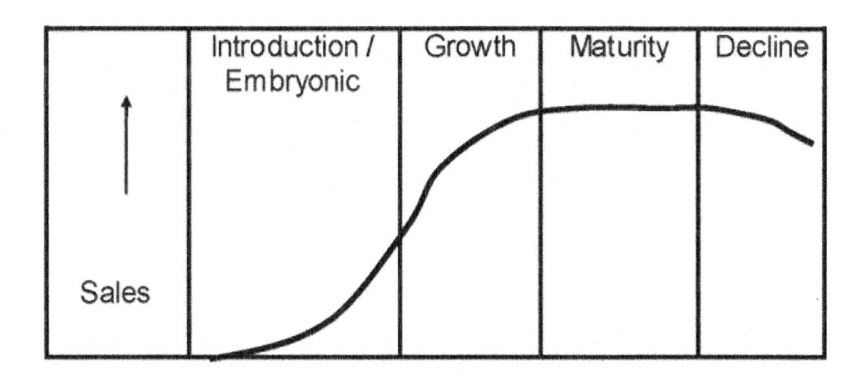

Sales ↑	Introduction / Embryonic	Growth	Maturity	Decline

There are several scenarios in the segment life cycle that will help shape NPD strategies:

1. **In the special case where the business segment life cycle is very short (let's say less than 18 months)** any company or brand that wants to remain relevant must constantly innovate.

Innovation is a cost of entry and a key part of the basis of competition. The type of innovations executed can run the full range, from lower level to disruptive. These are exciting businesses with constant change and with the potential for shifting brand share positions, including new brands entering, and existing brands leaving the segment. The current Smartphone war is a perfect example.

2. **If our business segment is in the early stages of a growth cycle and we are the marketer which caused the disruption,** then we need to support our NPD entry and build share.

3. **If our business segment is in the early stages of a growth cycle, and it is our competitor who caused the disruption**, then we had better quickly follow suit with our own NPD disruption, or be left behind with a dying brand. A fast follower entry with a me-too product can't be called a disruptive NPD, and it may or may not be adequate to maintain share position.

4. **If our business segment is in the mature or declining stages and we are satisfied to maintain position,** and willing to accept the uncertain risk of a competitive disruptive entry, we can pursue low level innovation programs, like renovations or line extensions.

5. **If our business segment is in the mature or declining stages and we want to seek a strategic move to re-energize sales and profits**, then executing a disruptive new product entry to re-cycle the business is not just appropriate, but very necessary.

6. **If we are contemplating the creation of an entirely new business segment, when there is no business life cycle curve to refer to,** then the launch of a new disruptive product is a mandatory pre-requisite.

THE ROLE OF DISRUPTIVE NEW PRODUCTS IN A COMPETITIVE STRATEGY

These last two scenarios are of particular importance to the focus of this book on searching for disruptive NPD ideas. We want to take a slow growth mature business and re-energize it by recycling it into an embryonic high growth stage, or we want to create an entirely new business segment or sub-segment. In either case, the need for disruptive NPD is the same if we are already one of the players or wish to enter this segment as a new player. Clearly, the other factors mentioned above must also support this strategy, regarding company strengths, resources, basis of competition, entry barriers, etc. A company must understand how these factors shape their overall template for NPD, and the merits of seeking disruptive new products.

The specific strategic move of launching a disruptive NPD product to recycle a business from its mature or declining stage to an embryonic stage is well established. It is one of many basic marketing facts and with countless successful examples:

- The liquid household cleaning segment as characterized by such products as Mr. Clean®, Spic and Span®, and Lysol®, was essentially mature when P&G re-energized it with their introduction of the disruptive new product innovation of Swiffer®. That product combined liquid household cleaners with a new form of mop that offers a far more convenient way to clean a floor vs. a mop and bucket of cleaning solution. Swiffer is now a huge success, adding significant sales volume to what was essentially a mature flat segment.

- Another example is in fever thermometry. Several years ago the business was essentially a lackluster mature segment with modest growth driven only by population growth. The launch of any new brand of mercury based fever thermometer to compete with Becton Dickinson®'s dominant BD® Fever Thermometer would not be worth it. Then, the application of new digital technology with faster read outs was applied to thermometry with new product launches. These launches, *by competition,* made the mercury thermometer obsolete, completely changed the competitive landscape, and recycled the business segment. And, with the premium pricing that consumers were willing to pay for the advanced benefits vs. the mercury thermometers, these new products increased the profitability of the marketers and the retailers. Since then we have seen another revolution in this segment with non-contact infrared technology with no need to disturb the child.

- Many years ago I recall using No-Doz® and Vivarin® to keep me awake during late night studies while in college. A sleepy category to be sure (no pun intended). Then Red Bull® Energy Drink, and 5-Hour Energy® and others took this sleepy segment and re-vitalized it (again no pun intended). Each of the new products sought to extend the benefits of the segment *from* just keeping you awake, *to* boosting energy and performance while you are awake. And, each product applied new formulations and packaging, to create a new sub-segment with premium pricing and huge sales volume.

- The walking cane business is as boring as they get. An immersion in this business would lead some marketers to run away. Not the folks at HurryCane® . They didn't look at the segment as it was. They looked at the segment for what it could be. Their re-invention of the walking cane with its new-to-the-world all terrain self-standing feature, drove HurryCane to become the #1 selling cane in America. I will leave it to the reader to imagine the next disruption in the walking cane business when smart technology is added. What would a smart walking cane do?

- The use of aluminum foil and / or clear plastic wrap for food protection was a segment with very modest growth aligned to

THE ROLE OF DISRUPTIVE NEW PRODUCTS IN A COMPETITIVE STRATEGY

population growth. Who would want to introduce a new competitive brand in this mature commodity segment? The answer: In 1959 Minigrip® manufactured the first self sealing plastic bag with a zipper. Then in 1968 Dow Chemical improved the function with their introduction of Ziploc® food storage bags for home use. Since then, many more advancements and brands followed and helped build this innovation into a very strong business segment. These folks took a quiet segment with little growth prospects and changed the paradigm for food storage and created an impressive new source for sales volume.

- When consumers seek relief from muscular and body aches and pains, they have a wide choice of OTC options including internal analgesics, topical analgesics, heating pads, etc. The OTC topical analgesics segment includes various rubs and creams with FDA approved ingredients that cause the perception of warmth when applied to the skin. Electric heating pads offer real warmth to the area, but prevent mobility. Both business segments were relatively mature until the launch of two new portable products, each with a new technology. Salonpas® Pain Relief Patches are single use disposable pads that contain some of the same ingredients as found in OTC topical cream analgesics, but in this new form they provide longer lasting warmth with less mess. The second innovation, also single use disposable, was developed by Thermacare® Heat Pads. These pads combine iron, oxygen, water and salts that react when exposed to the air to produce an exothermic heat producing effect. In a sense, both segments, the OTC topical analgesics and the electric heating pads, were recycled from mature to embryonic with the creation of this new sub-segment of portable heating pads.

- Very early in my career, I created disruption and growth in the first-aid elastic wrap business. The business of body wraps is focused on reducing the pain and swelling of body sprains and strains. The ACE® brand bandage dominated the business but had not innovated in years, and the segment showed slim growth. What I saw was an opportunity to drive disruption by creating a new-to-the-world sub-segment by adding value and new benefits to the wrap. At the time, when an individual experienced an injury, she would have to grab a bag of ice and place it over the wrapped joint to help relieve the pain and swelling. This was an inconvenient and messy affair, and did not encourage repeat use. I saw the merits of designing an elastic wrap with a built-in reusable cold gel pack (made cold by refrigerator storage) that provided cold and compression therapy, all in one product. This was a new-to-the-world device which was exactly the medically recommended first-aid **ICE** treatment for sprains and strains, i.e. **I**ce, **C**ompression, and **E**levation. The new ACE® Cold and Compression Wrap created incremental sales and at higher premium pricing.

These are but a few of the successful disruptive innovations that changed consumer behavior and revitalized a mature business into a high growth segment or new sub-segment. Some of these were examples by existing players within the segment, while others represented the strategic move by an outsider.

In summary, the approach to selecting the right NPD strategies for a company and for each of its operating segments starts with the strategic planning process. Once the overall strategic plan is set, it provides the foundation for determining the best NPD strategies for each business segment. There is a range to the types of NPD programs that may be chosen to support the strategic objectives for each segment. Each type of NPD initiative has its appropriate place within a competitive strategy, from low level renovations and line extensions, to disruptive new products.

THE ROLE OF DISRUPTIVE NEW PRODUCTS IN A COMPETITIVE STRATEGY

Within the strategic analysis and planning process, two key factors stand out in guiding a company towards the template of appropriate NPD strategies to pursue: 1) the company's brand share position within the landscape of the arena, and 2) the life cycle of that arena.

The execution of a disruptive NPD launch could represent either an offensive or defensive strategic move in helping a company support its overall competitive strategies. There are several strategic moves that stand out where disruptive NPD is appropriate and possibly necessary:

1. If the goal is to achieve a meaningful increase in revenue, then a disruptive NPD launch is one of several strategic moves to be considered.

2. For a company or brand that is in a dominant position within a segment, disruptive innovations may be necessary to help maintain their position.

3. If the goal is to re-energize and re-cycle a business from a mature or declining stage to a high growth embryonic stage, then a disruptive NPD launch is a necessary initiative for either a current player or non player.

4. For a company that seeks to gain significant share within one of their operating segments, then disruptive NPD is appropriate and possibly necessary.

5. For a company that wishes to enter a market new to them, disruptive NPD would be very necessary, and perhaps a prerequisite for success.

6. If the goal is to create a new-to-the-world segment, it is logical that it can only be done with a new disruptive NPD entry.

7. For a company that witnesses a competitive launch of a new disruptive product within one of its operating segments, then that company must follow suit with its own disruption, or be left behind.

The Vision Driving process as I describe in this book is a tool for creating a robust funnel of new disruptive NPD ideas that may offer the potential to fulfill one or more of the above strategic moves. Vision Driving can be viewed as one step in the pathway from a stated business objective, to the fulfillment of that objective. In simple terms the pathway might look like this:

Stated Business Objectives
> Specific Objective: Seek Strategic Move
> Requires Non-Linear Dramatic Change
> Possible Need for Disruption
> Possible Need for a Disruptive NPD Entry
> **Vision Driving NPD Ideation Process**
> Formulate Disruptive NPD Ideas
> Screen Ideas via NPD Stage-Gate process
> Select Disruptive NPD entry
> Execute Disruptive NPD launch
> **Achievement of Objectives**

Achieving a business objective via the execution of a successful disruptive NPD entry is one of the brass rings for any career. There are great challenges awaiting any individual or company which seeks to create a disruptive new product entry to support any of the strategic moves outlined above. The rewards are likewise great and well worth the journey for those with the courage to take the first steps. This book offers help. As stated in the title, it offers some new thinking, beyond the traditional NPD best practices on how to generate more and better disruptive new product ideas.

CHAPTER 2

The Funnel vs The Straw

Within the best practice approach to NPD there is a flow to the process, from the front end (sometimes called the fuzzy front end) where ideas are formulated, and then progressing through a series of stages and gates, delivering commercially viable launches at the end of the process.

When managed correctly, the process looks something like a funnel, whereas more ideas enter the front end, and fewer ideas emerge at the final end, screened and approved for launch.

Fuzzy Front End

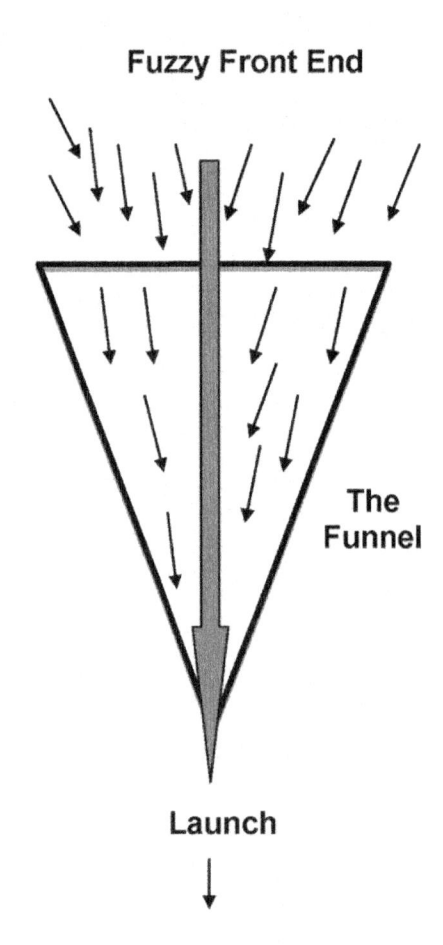

NPD Process of Stages & Gates

Ideas are formulated at the front end

Screening of ideas: typically via consumer research and technical feasibility

Selection of ideas to proceed to development

The Funnel

Screening of prototypes: consumer testing + manufacture + financial review + retailer interest

Pre-commercial approvals and plans: marketing + selling + financial

Launch

One essential requisite of a successful NPD function is a healthy number of ideas formulated at the front end. When there are just a few new product ideas at the front end of the funnel, the process of screening and selecting the right ideas becomes more challenging since the recourse for rejecting any ideas may leave the company with nothing else to pursue. I have too often heard management speak about "well if we don't pursue this, what else do we have?"

The NPD process is one of attrition, as the screening criteria are meant to weed out the weaker ideas. Without a robust volume of ideas in quantity

THE FUNNEL VS THE STRAW

and quality at the front end, there is a tendency to lower the screening hurdles and become married to the wrong ideas, for lack of any better alternatives. Wrong decisions are made and wrong ideas are pursued.

When there are too few ideas at the front end of the NPD process, the funnel looks more like a straw. Management places all their hopes in a few ideas and they assume that what goes in at the top will emerge at the bottom. One or two ideas at the front end of the NPD process in any business arena are too few. While the optimal number is not something we can specify, it is clear that the more ideas at the front end, the better the likelihood that the screening process will leave one or more ideas worthy of commercialization.

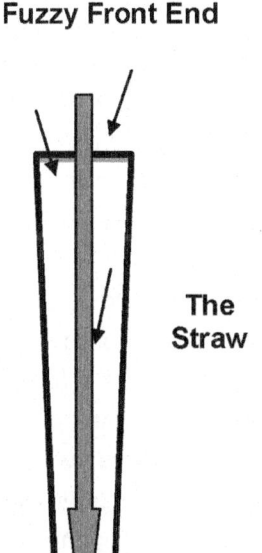

Fuzzy Front End

The Straw

Launch ?

The NPD process is dynamic, not static. At any given point the flow through the process should always have more ideas at the top, and fewer ideas downward through the stages.

This will ensure a steady flow of ideas and increase the likelihood that the ideas selected for launch will be good ideas and the right ideas for the company.

If instead, the NPD process looks more like a straw with a meager quantity of ideas, then there is a greater chance that a) no idea will emerge, or b) that any idea that emerges will be of lower quality in its measures against the Stage-Gate screening criteria.

SEARCHING OUTSIDE THE WHITE BOX FOR NEW PRODUCT INNOVATION

We want a robust funnel of ideas at the front end. This is not an easy task, which is why many companies fail to follow this logic, and then fail to achieve the NPD results that they want. It is a lot easier to come up with an idea or two, and assume that they will clear the Stage-Gate hurdles and emerge as commercially viable candidates.

As mentioned in the introduction, this funnel handicap in the NPD process is #5 on my short list of reasons for why many NPD functions go on to achieve disappointing results. Why is this so? Why don't more companies follow the logic of building a robust front end funnel of ideas?

I see several reasons:

A. An historical trend within the company to be satisfied with one or more low level innovation launches every year or so. In that respect, this particular company is not dissatisfied with their NPD process or results. They are meeting their expectations and doing fine, as long as their competitors don't overrun them with more aggressive initiatives.

B. A tendency to focus on an apparently good idea at the front end, to the exclusion of all others, for lack of motivation, support, or resources. We might hear staff say " *we have too many ideas....we need to focus* ". Instead of allowing the ideas to enter the funnel and the Stage-Gate® process where it would be vetted, management makes a premature judgment on some other basis. Ideas are cut before ever revealing their true worth.

C. Lack of a healthy, creative, and confident approach to idea formulation within the company. A company must believe in the importance of the funnel approach, they must believe that they can do it, and they must find and use methods that produce results for them.

D. Lack of courage and willingness to take on the difficult task that by its very nature forces risk and change within a company. Companies, like people, don't like change. Creating a robust front end of ideas is very difficult, can force change, can be a frustrating task, can consume a lot of energy, and yet still not produce good results. That's a tall order for any company.

The intent of this book is to offer a new approach to NPD idea formation that may help the solo entrepreneur or company team properly manage the front end of the funnel. By following this approach, the individual or company will have a better chance of improving both the quantity and quality of new NPD ideas entering the funnel of the Stage-Gate® process. This in turn will improve the odds that higher caliber products will pass through the screening stages and become commercial successes. My philosophy is that if a company recognizes the importance of creating a healthy front end funnel of ideas, and is willing to accept some change in the way they approach NPD idea formation, then they can improve their overall NPD launch success rate.

CHAPTER 3

What is the White Box ?

In many respects, the business goal of innovation and new product development is to find new ways, better ways, to satisfy consumer needs and generate profits. Achieving this goal depends on the successful linkage between consumer needs and the means to fulfill those needs. Greatest success comes from an optimized definition of the consumer need, and an optimized selection of technology to fulfill that need. It's a simple statement with great challenges.

Since each end of the connection, i.e. the need and the technology, is the result of selection processes, those processes used for uncovering, identifying, and selecting the need and the technology become vitally important to the success of the new product. Misjudgments in either will diminish the appeal and success of the innovation or new product. If the need is poorly defined how can we properly satisfy the real need? If the need is not completely defined how can we completely satisfy the consumer?

If the technology we use is fraught with safety issues, or is unfriendly to use, or of limited life, how can we expect the consumer to be happy with the product? If the technology is selected from what we are comfortable with and what we know, then how can we be sure it is optimal? And if the technology we choose to fulfill the consumer need is not optimal, how can we expect to optimize the potential for the new item? And, how can we defend against a competitor who leap frogs us by selecting the more advanced or optimized technology?

In the current world of best practices, the ideation process starts with the proper description of the consumer need. In theory, the need will then point us in the direction of how to satisfy the need, and the proper selection of the technology. As we delve more deeply into this whole process we will see that the current best practice for identifying needs has implicit limitations in helping us achieve the best new product ideas.

Current best practices for identifying consumer needs requires the unearthing of insights about consumer need-gaps within a segment, usually via consumer research. A need-gap is the difference between what the consumer says she wants or needs, and the level of fulfillment she receives from the available products.

In this type of research consumers are asked a series of questions about their product experience in a range of dimensions for benefits and attributes appropriate to the problem or need. These could include: Is it easy to use?, is it effective?, is it fast acting?, long lasting?, good value for the money?, comfortable?, easy to assemble?, is it portable?, good tasting?, attractive packaging?, etc. Each consumer answer is given on a scale where the highest number is complete satisfaction. Anything less than that is a need-gap. It is possible then, that for each dimension we can learn where the consumer is not fulfilled, and hence where the need-gaps are.

When the consumer responds to these questions, she is thinking about two points on a mental graph: what I really want, and what I am currently getting.

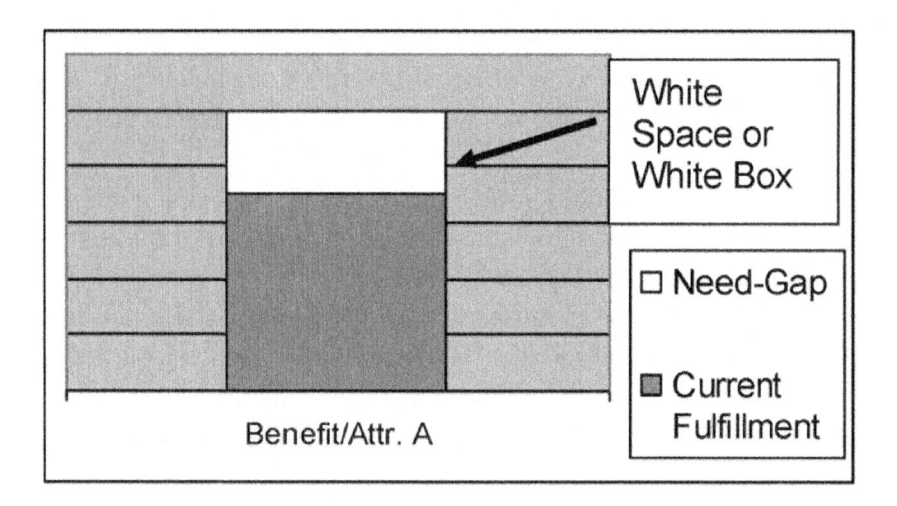

◀ SEARCHING OUTSIDE THE WHITE BOX FOR NEW PRODUCT INNOVATION

[Figure: Bar chart showing Benefit/Attr. A with legend indicating White Space or White Box (arrow pointing to white area at top of bar), Need-Gap, and Current Fulfillment.]

In this graph the height (in rating) of the top of the white bar, is equal to what the consumer really wants. The height of the dark bar is her current level of satisfaction. The difference is her need-gap. Often times this need-gap is referred to as a White Space or as I call it, the White Box.

In theory, the gaps will point to opportunities for businesses to pursue. This is where consumers still have unmet needs waiting for a new product to fulfill that need. Marketers are looking for White Box opportunities. When comprehensive research is conducted, the profile of the White Box opportunity is shaped from the long list of questions and their answers. The profile might suggest that there are still unmet needs for a faster acting product, or one that is easier to use on the go, or with a more comfortable grip, or with a longer battery life, etc.

WHAT IS THE WHITE BOX?

This profile can look something like this, revealing the full range of possible White Spaces or White Boxes.

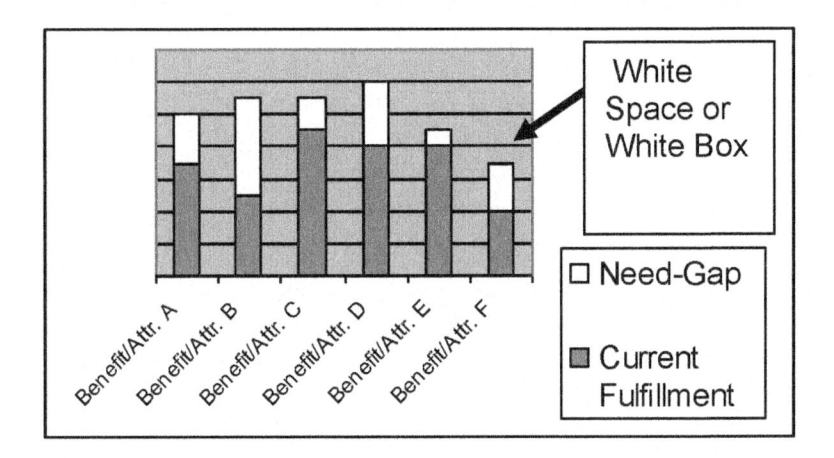

[Chart showing bars for Benefit/Attr. A through Benefit/Attr. F, with legend indicating White Space or White Box, Need-Gap, and Current Fulfillment]

This type of research implicitly accepts the notion that the consumer comes to the survey with his own idea of what his ideal satisfaction would be, and separately, his current experience within the category. The former is a mental construct by the consumer of what the perfect world solution might be. It is an upper limit of what the consumer envisions as the perfect world solution for each benefit or attribute.

This is the fundamental limitation of this best practice approach to identifying consumer needs. This construct is limited by the consumer's understanding of the current world as he sees it and or envisions it. The consumer's sense of the ideal is limited by his vision and wishes. His linear vision of an ideal solution cannot see over the hills of his reality. In turn, this approach will affect the entire NPD process, producing new product ideas that are more likely to be linear extensions of the existing, rather than disruptive ideas that change the paradigm of the business.

SEARCHING OUTSIDE THE WHITE BOX FOR NEW PRODUCT INNOVATION

The smart marketer is able to look beyond this White Box in pursuit of disruptive new product ideas. This is the focus in this book. We should not expect the consumer to lead us towards disruptive new product ideas. This should be our job.

CHAPTER 4

White Box Limitations

As mentioned, the size of the need-gap White Space or White Box is defined by the upper limit of what the consumer envisions as the perfect world solution for that particular benefit / attribute question in the survey. As also mentioned, this vision is limited by her grounding in the current world and her capacity to envision the optimal solution to her needs. This limitation in the consumer's vision establishes an upper boundary of the size and profile of the White Box that a marketer would pursue.

Consumer Boundary of Desired Expectations

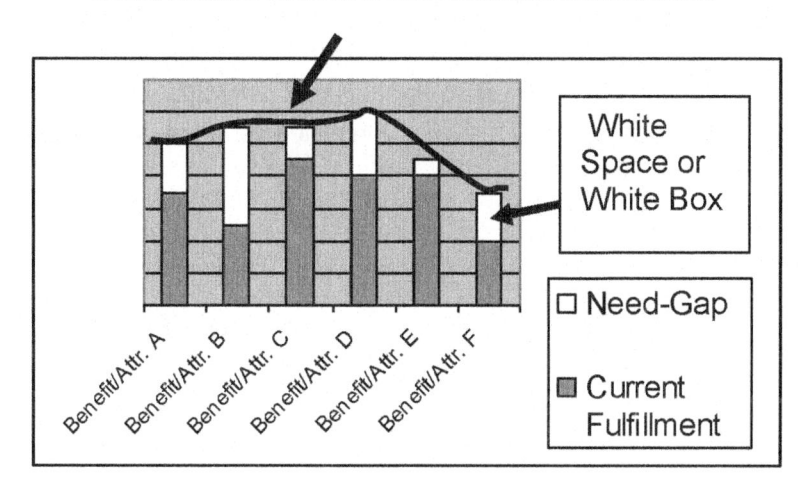

- White Space or White Box
- ☐ Need-Gap
- ■ Current Fulfillment

Benefit/Attr. A, Benefit/Attr. B, Benefit/Attr. C, Benefit/Attr. D, Benefit/Attr. E, Benefit/Attr. F

SEARCHING OUTSIDE THE WHITE BOX FOR NEW PRODUCT INNOVATION

When the marketer continues the process of connecting needs with technologies, these limitations to the White Space need-gaps then limit the selection of technology connections, and ultimately the appeal and success of the new product.

This need-gap best practice approach to NPD will lead to new ideas that may be linear in their advancement vs the creation of some new paradigm. Such research will typically lead to making old ways better vs. the scrapping of old ways for entirely new ways. Understanding this limitation and its implication on the whole NPD process is vital to the goal of developing the most successful and profitable innovations.

When we speak about disruptive NPD ideas, we are speaking about ideas that break the linear trend of an existing paradigm. These ideas disrupt the way we do things, and disrupt the landscape of products and services that existed within that paradigm. Successful disruptive ideas change the world in small to big ways, and in so doing, create tremendous pathways to revenue and profit growth. The smartest marketers understand this. These are the NPD ideas that marketers hope to pursue....*if they have the courage.*

Disruptive ideas do not come from this need-gap White Box research. If we want to pursue them we must learn how to look beyond the boundaries of current White Box analyses. If we want to exceed the competition then we must move beyond the best practices employed by our competition.

WHITE BOX LIMITATIONS

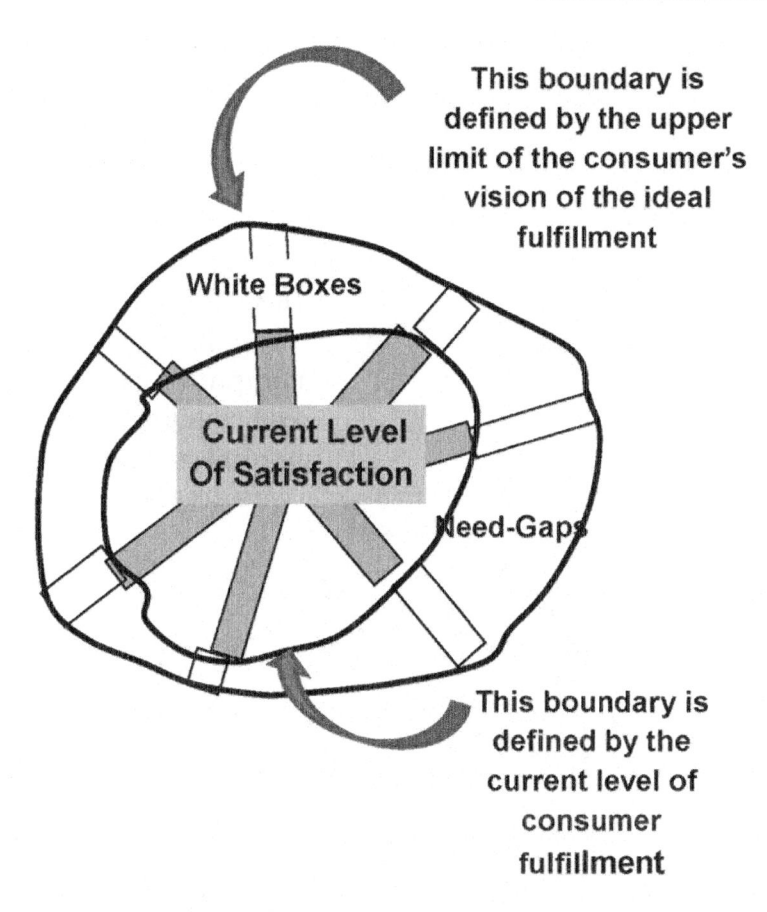

This boundary is defined by the upper limit of the consumer's vision of the ideal fulfillment

White Boxes

Current Level Of Satisfaction

Need-Gaps

This boundary is defined by the current level of consumer fulfillment

White Box need-gap analysis is a place to start the process of identifying the optimal consumer need. It is not the end of the process. In theory, if we can extend the boundary of consumer expectations then we can expand the need-gaps and expand the profile and magnitude of the appeal in a new product.

Disruptive ideas do this by extending into the "Expansion Space" beyond the White Box. The new ideas literally create the Expansion Space. This is where disruptive new products, game changers, or paradigm shifts change our world. No one thought it could exist. No consumer was able to describe it from his linear vision. No consumer thought he needed it until it was there. And no consumer felt wanting for not having it.

SEARCHING OUTSIDE THE WHITE BOX FOR NEW PRODUCT INNOVATION

Disruptive ideas are those ideas that satisfy consumer needs that consumers did not know they had, and could not articulate. These ideas do not emerge from the traditional need-gap research, and the ideas do not reside in the White Box. They create and reside in the Expansion Space.

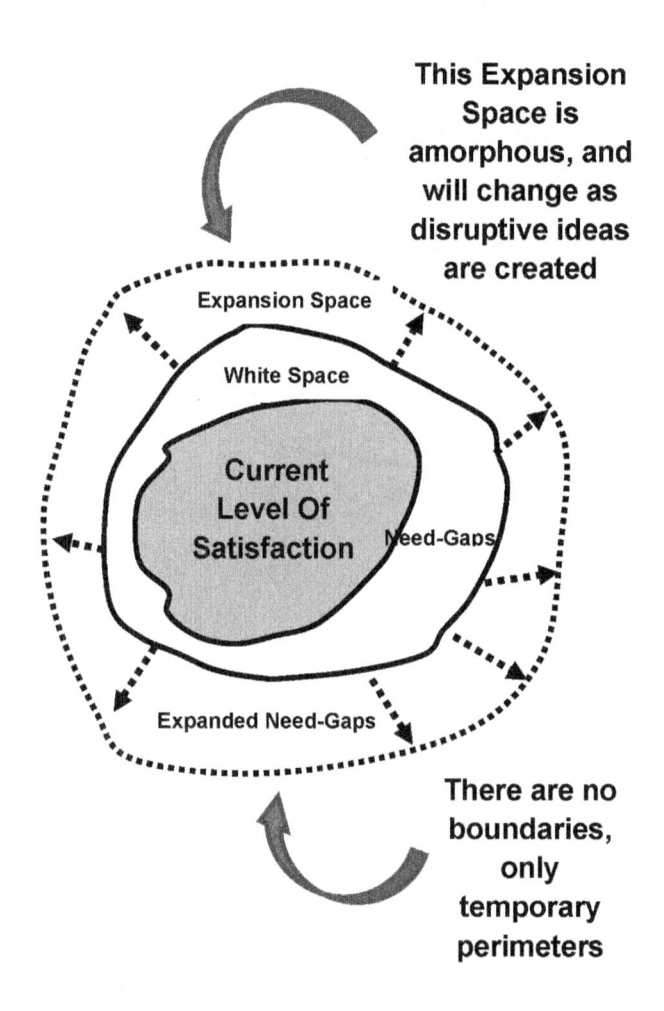

This Expansion Space is amorphous, and will change as disruptive ideas are created

Expansion Space

White Space

Current Level Of Satisfaction

Need-Gaps

Expanded Need-Gaps

There are no boundaries, only temporary perimeters

WHITE BOX LIMITATIONS

Question: If the most innovative ideas reside in the Expansion Space, how do we create this space and explore it for ideas?

Answer: The paradox is that it is the idea itself that creates the Expansion Space and the new need-gaps that did not previously exist. The Expansion Space does not exist until a new disruptive idea is formulated. Contrary to White Space searches for new ideas which seek to unearth need-gap insights from consumer research to drive ideation, in this approach it is the new idea itself that drives the expansion of the need gap.

Disruptive innovations change the consumer's expectations about how they can meet their fundamental needs and advances the boundaries of what they perceive as the ideal solution.

People end up wanting something that their existing wants could not articulate. Once presented with the new product, all of their prior beliefs about wants and fulfillment are forever altered.

The world changes in small or big ways as the new paradigm takes hold. Disruption caused by new products is one of the pathways of what we call progress.

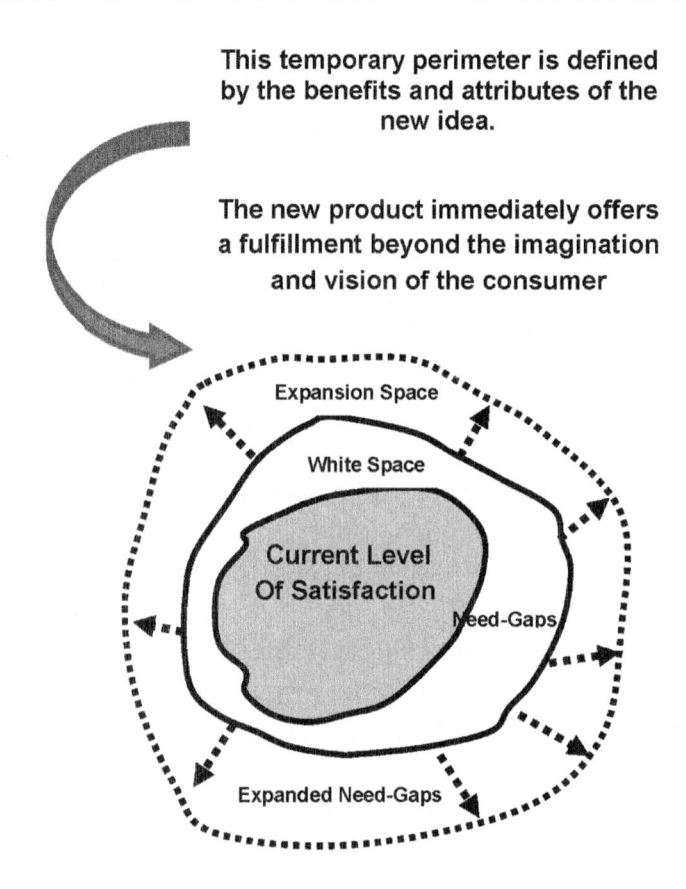

SEARCHING OUTSIDE THE WHITE BOX FOR NEW PRODUCT INNOVATION

This temporary perimeter is defined by the benefits and attributes of the new idea.

The new product immediately offers a fulfillment beyond the imagination and vision of the consumer

- Expansion Space
- White Space
- Current Level Of Satisfaction
- Need-Gaps
- Expanded Need-Gaps

As previously mentioned, there is a range to the effects of disruption and disruptive new products. At the highest end, the invention of the telescope changed more than the field of astronomy. It changed the way mankind viewed his place within the universe. The telephone changed more than the way people communicated. It changed the nature of relationships, business, warfare, and a whole lot more.

On the lower end of disruption, are the new products that changed behavior and attitudes that were limited to the segment or business arena. The introduction of fabric softeners forever changed consumers' expectations about how their washed garments should feel. Until the advent of color TV, consumers were content to view the world in black and white. If queried in research they might have said they wanted a larger screen, better audio, or better programming, (White Box need-gaps). Once color TV was shown to people, their needs changed, and black and white TVs were history.

In our time, this notion about the creation of NPD ideas in the Expansion Space and the effect it has on consumer needs was best articulated and demonstrated by *Steve Jobs*. He went so far as to say that he didn't like to conduct consumer research because he could not expect them to see beyond their reality. *Steve Jobs* clearly put Apple's attention into a vision that created the Expansion Space for Apple and its consumers. Apple's innovations changed the way people "solved" various problems or needs and thus marginalized many existing paradigms along the way. The consumer's needs changed on each day of a new Apple launch.

When we speak about the White Box limitations, we can see the limitations on both ends of NPD ideas, ie the need – technology combination. First, from the above discussion, we can see that a need-gap approach to new product ideation has limitations on defining the optimal need. But second, it also places limitations *to the technology we seek to satisfy that need*. Why? Because by its nature the need-gap White Box approach does not force the consumer to see beyond his world for need fulfillment by technologies or novel applications that he is unaware of. In turn, this approach does not stretch our search for, or creation of, new technology or new technology applications. We would not search for a technology solution for a need that we were unable to identify.

There is another reason that the traditional need-gap White Box approach is unlikely to drive us towards disruptive technology or disruptive technology applications. The company that adheres to the traditional White Box approach is also most likely to have a mindset that restricts them from searching for new disruptive technologies. We

SEARCHING OUTSIDE THE WHITE BOX FOR NEW PRODUCT INNOVATION

can credit Professor *Clayton Christensen* in his book *The Innovator's Dilemma* for providing another perspective on this. He maintains that many companies are implicitly tied to their current paradigms, including associated technologies, so that their search for disruptive change is less likely. These companies have a vested interest in leveraging their current paradigm in skills and assets in seeking better ways of satisfying consumer needs. They are seeking better ways to achieve a competitive advantage, but tend to explore linear advancements as opposed to disruptive changes.

Going a step further, such companies do not want to employ a new technology that may antiquate and marginalize their assets and competitive strengths with existing technology. How many times have we seen a company that was so wedded to its infrastructure and paradigm that it was unable or unwilling to embrace disruptive change that eventually put them out of business? Kodak actually invented digital photography but was unable to create a business model to replace their very profitable film based business. They struggled with fears of cannibalization as others seized the day and drove the world into digital photography. Kodak filed for bankruptcy in 2012.

Such companies will not be inclined to search for NPD technology outside of the White Box. They may be aware of new technologies, but are not likely to seek them out because it means vast changes to their way of doing business. The company that makes the best OTC sunscreen lotion may have a disincentive to exploring NPD ideas that require new, non-OTC Drug technology paradigms. It is more likely that their search would look for new ways to make it easier to apply a lotion, or create a lotion with longer lasting protection, or protection from salt water or chlorine water, or less greasy, and so on. But such a company would not consider a battery operated "magic wand" technology that provides a sun protective energy field to the skin, because it is outside their comfort zone.

WHITE BOX LIMITATIONS

The business paradigm of this OTC Drug company does not encourage it to invest in something that will circumvent or close down their current skills and assets in OTC Drugs. That company, like many others in OTC Drugs, spends its time looking for improvements to their current product line. Making it faster acting, stronger, longer lasting, better tasting, easier to swallow, easier to apply, all become the mantras of their OTC Drug technology searches. They are not looking to replace their paradigm, but instead are looking to improve it. Sadly, as *Clayton Christensen* has suggested, they can do all the right things in their business, and yet still be put out of business by a competitor that went outside their comfort zone for a new paradigm solution. If the idea of an electronic magic wand that provides skin sun protection ever becomes a reality, the OTC sun protection skin lotions may be put out of business.

When a company restricts its NPD search for new product ideas to within the White Box AND restricts its interest in technologies to within their existing comfort zone, we should not expect to see them create disruptive NPD ideas.

If we are to pursue more disruptive NPD ideas, then we need to search beyond the limitations of the White Box, and we must be open to changing our current paradigm comfort zone. We must learn how to search in the Expansion Space.

CHAPTER 5

The Vision Driving Process - Searching in the Expansion Space

The challenge then is how to create disruptive NPD ideas if they don't come from traditional need-gap White Box research.

Answer: **Unlike the White Box analysis, these new ideas come from the Ideator's vision, not from the consumer's existing need-gaps. Once knowing and accepting this, we are encouraged to look beyond the White Box for truly disruptive ideas. We are encouraged to search outside The White Box!**

So, how do we conduct this search?

The search method that takes us beyond the White Boxes into the Expansion Space is what I call *"Vision Driving ™"*, a mental journey that forces the emergence of disruptive ideas. Vision Driving follows many paths, sometimes separately, sometimes combined, with the intent on leading to disruptive thinking and disruptive ideas.

This process has existed historically, although not by this name. It has taken many forms, sometimes without apparent structure, and sometimes without conscious intent. There are times when this process has

THE VISION DRIVING PROCESS - SEARCHING IN THE EXPANSION SPACE

taken months or years, and other times it has taken minutes in what looked like a moment of eureka. Sometimes it has been a solo experience and other times a collaborative experience. The Vision Driving process as I describe it is based on historical successes, and then builds on it to make it applicable to our purposes.

Our intent is to learn from history, learn the key motives and elements to the innovation process, understand how they worked, and then build on this to create a usable guide for searching and creating disruptive ideas in the Expansion Space. We will first look at the broad basis for all innovations, and then look at a range of some specific innovations for clues on how they happened. Our objective is to deconstruct the possible steps that led to these innovations, and then isolate those factors that seem to reoccur as possible stimuli, so that we can apply them going forward in the Vision Driving process.

At the very foundation of all innovation is man's desire to satisfy one or more human needs. Throughout mankind's history of inventing and innovation is our desire to seek better ways to satisfy a range of human needs. These needs are best described by Abraham Maslow in his special theory of behavioral psychology. In his 1943 paper *"A Theory of Human Motivation",* in the *Psychological Review"* he provided a framework for observing and understanding human behavior and motivation. Maslow believed that there were 5 stages of human needs that motivate all human behavior. His theory, often referred to as Maslow's Need Hierarchy, described each stage, from basic needs to self actualization, and suggested that there was a progression in seeking need fulfillment from the basic needs to the highest needs. Maslow believed that as a person satisfies a need at one level, he moves up the hierarchy to seek fulfillment at the next higher level. This progression is often depicted as a pyramid.

Maslow's Need Hierarchy

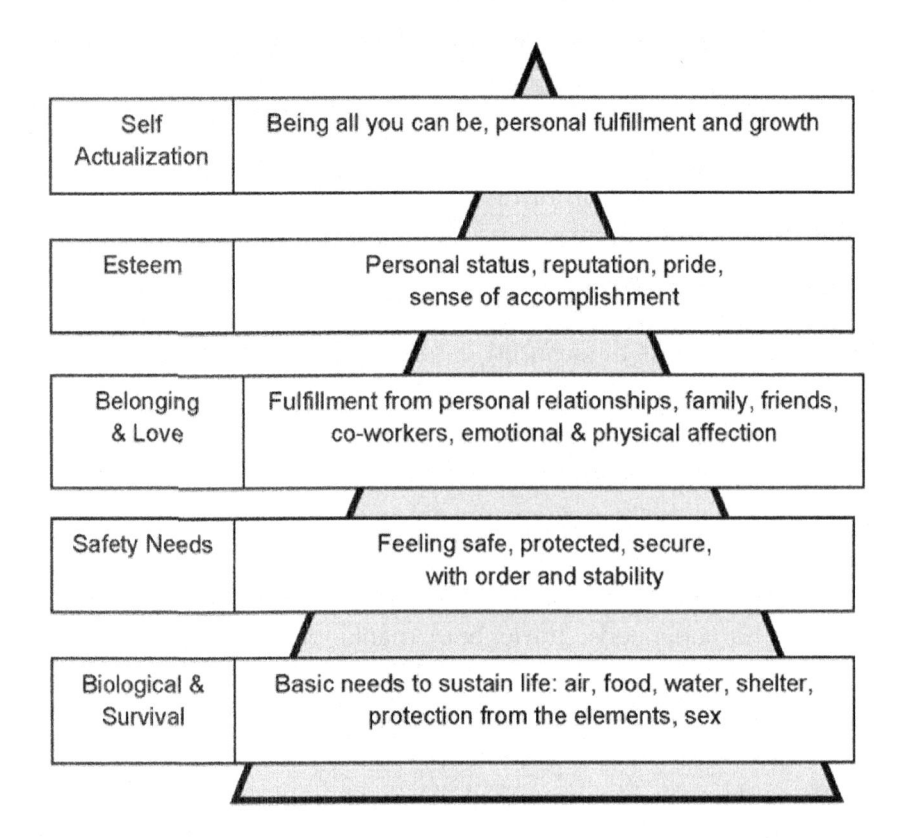

Self Actualization	Being all you can be, personal fulfillment and growth
Esteem	Personal status, reputation, pride, sense of accomplishment
Belonging & Love	Fulfillment from personal relationships, family, friends, co-workers, emotional & physical affection
Safety Needs	Feeling safe, protected, secure, with order and stability
Biological & Survival	Basic needs to sustain life: air, food, water, shelter, protection from the elements, sex

My perspective on Maslow's Need Hierarchy is not so much about how individuals progress up the pyramid as they satisfy lower level needs, but more about how products and services satisfy the various levels of needs. It's a different take on Maslow's Need Hierarchy, and helps us understand how innovations meet our needs, and why they gained acceptance.

Every product or service conceived by man satisfies one or more of Maslow's needs. Every advancement, every invention, and every innovation by mankind was motivated in some way by need fulfillment at one or more of these stages. And, every future advancement will

THE VISION DRIVING PROCESS - SEARCHING IN THE EXPANSION SPACE

likewise be in response to, or support some type of need fulfillment on Maslow's Hierarchy. Since our goal is to learn the full range of motives and stimuli that can help us create new disruptive NPD ideas, then it is essential for us to be grounded in this insight.

An innovation may not actually satisfy a Maslow need, but rather, it may provide a better means to achieving that need fulfillment. In this way, a product or service may be an adjunct to achieving need fulfillment. The automobile didn't feed us or keep us warm, but it sure helps us retrieve things that do feed us and keep us warm. Also, a product or service may satisfy multiple levels of needs. A car can be different things to different people, as they view the car from different need levels. A car can help us secure **Basic** human needs, help us stay **Safe** from the elements during travel or to help us quickly flee for safety from danger, or it can help us maintain **Relationships** with family and friends, or can be stylish enough to help us improve our **Esteem** in the "community".

The business of household cleaning supplies and devices would not at first seem like a segment that can satisfy most of Maslow's needs, but it does. A clean home can help preserve and protect our home as one of our most **Basic** needs for shelter. A clean home can also help us meet our **Safety** needs by protecting us from the elements like bugs, germs, or rain storms that could do us harm. If we are single and invite someone new to our home for a drink, it would help if the home were inviting and clean, to help us build our new found relationship and achieve our need for **Relationships and Love**. And finally, we all know that a clean home reflects on us in such a way that when the home is clean and seen as clean, it helps elevate our sense of pride, our reputation, and sense of **Esteem.**

A rather far out example involves the purchase of melons. If you are like me, the selection of a sweet melon is a combination of touch, smell, and luck. Some time ago I had invented the idea of a hand held non-invasive melon sweetness tester that could help a shopper select the best melon for her family. Clearly the melon tester would be an adjunct to helping a mom satisfy her family's **Basic** need for food. But when we look at the process that a mom might go through from the time she selects a melon for purchase, to the time she serves it at the dinner table, we might see something else. When she is able to buy and serve a melon that is just right in its sweetness and ripeness, her family is delighted and grateful to her for her "melon picking skills", and for this, she is proud. The melon tester has helped this mom feel a small sense of pride. She has achieved something grand, and received the adulation from her family. The melon tester would be able to satisfy her Maslow need for **Self Esteem and Pride.**

The personal computer and the internet don't feed us, but they help us at business, personal, and societal levels in working more productively, and / or living more happily, in satisfying all our needs. These innovations were clearly disruptive in the way they helped fulfill every need on the Maslow Need Hierarchy.

Any innovation can be mapped against the Maslow Hierarchy to reveal which needs are or could be fulfilled. The exercise becomes useful as a first step in helping us understand the connections between a business arena and its reason for being in satisfying the hierarchy of human needs. And, by pressure testing each level of need against our business arena, we may actually find new opportunities for innovations that might extend our range of need fulfillment.

Examples of innovations vs Maslow's Need Hierarchy

Self Actualization	Oral Contraceptives, Personal Computer, Ballpoint Pen, Eyeglasses, Gun Powder/Firearms
Esteem	Personal computer, Automobile, Botox® Cosmetics, Brassiere, Gun Powder/Firearms
Belonging & Love	Automobile, Personal Computer, Oral Contraceptives, Botox® Cosmetics, Ballpoint Pen, Brassiere
Safety Needs	Needle & Thread, Automobile, Oral Contraceptives, Personal Computer, Aspirin, Air Conditioning, Eyeglasses, Gun Powder/Firearms
Biological & Survival	Needle & Thread, Automobile, Oral Contraceptives, Personal Computer, Ballpoint Pen, Aspirin, Eyeglasses, Air Conditioning, Gun Powder/Firearms

Maslow's Need Hierarchy is pretty much an accepted insight into human behavior. For us it becomes helpful in our quest to uncover the motives and stimuli that drive innovations. As we look forward to any business arena where we want to execute an NPD program, our initial questions about Maslow's need fulfillment will help us open our minds to our business, where it is today, and where it could be tomorrow.

SEARCHING OUTSIDE THE WHITE BOX FOR NEW PRODUCT INNOVATION

- Which of Maslow's needs are satisfied or could be satisfied, either directly or indirectly by our business?

- Which of those needs do we currently focus on? Which do we ignore? Are we making the right selection decisions to optimize our franchise and sales?

- How is our business positioned to satisfy these needs?

- How can we, or should we expand our business definition?

- Does this review help point us in the direction of NPD ideation? Where might NPD offer the greatest return?

Next, in our search to uncover the stimuli that might have driven historical innovations, we want to go much deeper than the Maslow study of needs. We want to uncover stimuli that were more specific to the task. We want to identify the stimuli that contributed to the inspiration and configuration of the new idea itself. And we want to understand if there are a set of reoccurring stimuli that were at play. Our objective in building the Vision Driving process is to see how we can use these same stimuli proactively in helping us create new NPD ideas.

To uncover these stimuli we can look at a range of historical inventions and innovations. Man's progress can in some way be viewed on a series of innovation pathways: A very brief list of such pathways might include:

- Tools: from primitive stone tools, to metal tools, moveable tools, mechanical tools, electrical, pneumatic, hydraulic, lasers.

- Harnessing power: from manual manpower, to the use of animals, using nature as in running water and wind, steam

THE VISION DRIVING PROCESS - SEARCHING IN THE EXPANSION SPACE

power, internal combustion engine, electric motors, jet engines, solar, nuclear.

- Distant communications: starting with fire, drums, smoke, flags, horse drawn messengers, telegraph, telephone, the internet, cell phones, video chatting.

- Illumination: starting with the nighttime wood fire, the fire torch, use of animal fat and wicks in clay pots, oil lamps, candles, gaslights, electric light bulb, fluorescent bulbs, LEDs.

If we were to dissect these pathways to identify the mental processes that drove these innovations, we might see different stimuli that were factors at different times along the historical pathway, some of which could include:

- A motivation to satisfy one or more human needs.

- A vision by the innovator or inventor to see beyond the obvious.

- Access to pre-knowledge on the subject, and awareness of trends.

- A technological borrowing, combining, and building on prior methods and knowledge.

- Ability to observe a behavior, whether within the studied subject or from outside the subject, discover some new insight, and then apply it.

This provides a good general starting point to understanding the innovation process, but we want to go deeper into specific examples.

◄ SEARCHING OUTSIDE THE WHITE BOX FOR NEW PRODUCT INNOVATION

If we asked people prior to the 1800's how a horse drawn carriage could be improved (as if we were seeking the White Space need-gaps) they might have answered: " I want a faster horse, easier access into the carriage, more comfortable seats ". It was Henry Ford in fact who is credited with the quote: "If I had asked people what they wanted, they would have said 'faster horses' "

Would people have said "I want to replace the horse with a mechanized horse"? It's unlikely they would have asked for this because they were unaware of its possibility. Most people were not aware of engines that might be suitable for replacing the horse, and could not envision the application. They could not look beyond their own world to see the next. They were not dissatisfied with the limitations of a horse because they could not yet envision a better solution.

The automobile did not come from consumer research into White Spaces of the available means of mobility at the time. The idea for the automobile came not from a chorus of consumers asking for it, but rather from those inventors who had the vision. They saw the need for improvement in personal mobility and saw the opportunity for applying alternate means (technology) to solving the problem.

A German, Karl Benz, is generally believed to be the inventor of the modern automobile. He was an inventor that made use of the internal combustion engine in a variety of applications. For him, the application of these engines to a self-managed means of mobility was obvious. He understood the human need for mobility and recognized how a self-operated motorized vehicle could greatly expand man's abilities beyond just getting from place to place faster.

Whether structured or not, and whether conscious or not, the ideation process for the creation of automobiles may have included some or all of these factors:

- Having the belief that human mobility could be improved, and making the decision to pursue the solution.

- Understanding where a self-managed personal mobility device satisfied multiple human needs.

- Challenging existing beliefs:

    o That a horse was required for personal mobility.

    o That speedy mobility required that others decide on when you can go, where you can go, and with whom you must go (ie mass transit trains of the time).

- Applying emerging technology (internal combustion engine) to personal mobility.

- Borrowing one solution for mass mobility (motorized trains) to personalized mobility.

- Building, borrowing, and combining a long list of previous innovations in engineering, chemistry, metallurgy, as so forth.

Staying with mobility for the moment, let's look at the invention of roller skates. It's a rather simple device that remains with us today. The first patented roller skate was introduced in 1760 and has seen improvements and growing use since then. How was it invented? And the more interesting question, why was it invented?

Did the inventor ask people who wore shoes, how they would like to improve shoes? Doubtful. And if he did, what would they say? Can we even imagine people saying that they want roller wheeled shoes?

SEARCHING OUTSIDE THE WHITE BOX FOR NEW PRODUCT INNOVATION

One story suggests that roller skates were first invented in Holland by a man who wanted to apply the benefits of ice skating as a means of winter mobility, to all season land mobility. He built wooden wheels on a tiny cart that attached to the bottom of shoes. Over the years improvements were made in design, functional attributes such as turning and stopping control, ease of wearing, speed, appearance, etc. In October, 2014 we heard about one more advancement with the creation of *RocketSkates* as invented by *Peter Treadway* who saw the merits of combining battery powered motorization to the roller skate platform.

The original inventor had the vision of "gliding" along land the same way ice skating was a means for gliding along ice. He made the mental leap from ice to land, and then had the creativity to imagine combining wheels with shoes to make land "gliding" possible. Whether conscious or not, this ideation process may have included some or all of these factors:

- Deciding to improve personalized land mobility.

- Observing the behavior of ice skating as a "gliding" mobility experience.

- Making the mental leap from ice to land with the idea of borrowing the gliding experience.

- Challenging existing beliefs: who said you can't skate in summer or on land?

- Borrowing technology, eg wheels used in carts & carriages.

- Applying miniaturization of wheeled carts to the feet.

Although roller skates seem obvious today, it was not so obvious the day before they were invented.

THE VISION DRIVING PROCESS - SEARCHING IN THE EXPANSION SPACE

My favorite example of Vision Driving ideation in mobility is the invention of wheeled luggage. I often ask people: "How long has the wheel been around?" Then I ask: "How long has luggage been around?" Finally I ask : " How long has wheeled luggage been around?" What is striking in the answers is the fact that the combination of wheels with luggage could have occurred thousands of years ago, thousands of years before their actual invention. But that did not happen. In fact it was invented just in the past 45 years.

There are two stories that lead to the invention of wheeled luggage. In the first we see that with the emergence of air travel, there was a greater need to haul luggage around. And interestingly, the people doing most of the hauling were pilots and flight attendants. They were the lead groups of people who had a greater need for improved convenience. What they did was to buy small hand trucks and put their luggage onto them. Now they could convert from hauling luggage to wheeling their luggage. So much better! It wouldn't take much for luggage manufacturers to notice this make-shift behavior and make the leap to combining wheels onto the bottoms of existing luggage designs. This was followed by the evolution of luggage to today's roll-abouts.

The other story suggests that one individual, Bernard D. Sadow, invented wheeled luggage in 1970. It happened as he was hauling his own luggage while at the same time noticing a worker using a wheeled cart to move heavy machinery. Bingo! He put the two together and invented wheeled luggage.

In either case we are closer to knowing the possible stimuli used in making this invention:

- Deciding to overcome the personal pain and frustration of hauling luggage.

SEARCHING OUTSIDE THE WHITE BOX FOR NEW PRODUCT INNOVATION

- Observing and borrowing behavior.

    o From make-shift behavior among lead groups under study (frequent travelers, eg airline workers).

    o From a different group and different scenario (the guy pushing a cart).

- Challenging existing beliefs: who said luggage can't have wheels?

- Growing trend in the appeal and use of air travel created a greater need to haul luggage around.

- Borrowing and combining technology, e.g. applying wheels as used in carts to the bottom of luggage.

- Miniaturization: If we imagine a very small wheeled cart, it begins to look like wheeled luggage.

In another aspect of mobility and transportation we see the recent emergence of bike sharing programs in big cities, notably in New York City. So far this program seems like a success. Why so? What are the factors that drove this innovation?

- Growing trend in sharing, both in the virtual world, as in texting, skyping, Facebook® and photo sharing such as Snapfish, ShutterflyA®, etc, and in the real world such as car sharing as Car2Go® and Zipcar®.

- Growing congestion in big cities where population is growing without similar growth in transportation infrastructure.

THE VISION DRIVING PROCESS - SEARCHING IN THE EXPANSION SPACE

- Increased interest in "going green" and concerns for greenhouse effects produced by cars, buses, etc.

- The fact that big cities don't offer most individuals much space to store their own bikes.

- Increased trend towards individuals with multiple part time jobs forcing greater use of quick transportation during the work day.

- Borrowing from the success of car sharing programs.

One of the most influential innovations was the invention of photography. Its impact was broad and still growing to this day. The invention of photography is actually a series of inventions that started in the early 1800's, with the observation that certain chemicals will change color in the presence of light. At first very crude, and then with refinements, the process evolved towards the use of some form of silver coated plate or substrate that captured images as the light hitting the surface altered the color of the substrate. The invention was the combination of advances in chemistry and optics, which continues to this day. This was a disruptive innovation that affected a full range of human activity, including: business, science, engineering, family relationships, government controls, law enforcement, art, military campaigns, and on. What do we suspect were the key stimuli in driving this innovation?

- Man's innate desire to record his actions and progress in history, as starting with the art of cave dwellers depicting their animal hunts, as driven by ego and pride (**Esteem** on the Maslow Need Hierarchy).

- Increased need for low cost portrait images to satisfy the needs for **Esteem** and **Relationships** with the masses, as opposed to portrait oil painting which was available only for the elite.

- Borrowing the behavior of plant life in noticing how sunlight caused a chemical reaction in the leaf.

- Combining the chemical oxidation effect of silver with paper.

- Borrowing the technology of the lens.

- Combining technology of optics and chemistry.

- Imaginative mind tools in wondering if and how sunlight can be put to work by man on a man made substrate.

- Trend at the time for more scientific investigation, knowledge and precision.

- Trend towards industrialization and the need for reproducible images.

The modern refrigerator had its beginnings in the early 1800's as various people were experimenting with the phenomenon that as a liquid converts to a gas, it expands and draws heat from its environment. This dynamic was observed and described mathematically by the works of several scientists including Boyle and Charles. Various devices were created that forced a fluid through a closed pipe loop from a condensed liquid state where it released heat to the ambient, to an expanding gaseous state where it absorbed ambient heat. As the process repeats itself with a series of pumps, compressors, and coils, it provides a cooling benefit to the desired chamber. This series of inventions and advancements in refrigeration may have been driven by a number of factors:

- As the industrial revolution continued its advances, there was a growing trend of people migrating from rural farms to the cities where the factories were, leaving them at a distance from food sources. This trend fostered the greater need for food preservation.

- Challenging the belief that man cannot create cold from that which is non-cold.

- Borrowing the insight and mathematics of gaseous behavior from scientists like Boyles and Charles.

- Combining the various advances in the engineering of valves and pumps, as well as the growing use and applications of electricity as a power source.

The sewing machine as we know it today had gone through a number of variations by two individuals who are credited with the invention, Elias Howe and Isaac Merritt Singer. Developed in the mid 1800's, the sewing machine revolutionized the garment making process, and helped to create the garment industry. Some of the factors leading to the innovation might have included:

- Man's **Basic** need for clothing.

- Challenging the belief that the productivity of sewing could be achieved only by adding more or faster hand seamstresses.

- Observing, dissecting, and then borrowing and translating the manual human sewing activity into a mechanical one.

- Growing trend in office work that helped increase the demand for a low cost clothing wardrobe.

Breakfast cereals may not look like an innovation, but it was an important one that is still with us today. What were the circumstances that led to this innovation? During the mid 19th century the American

SEARCHING OUTSIDE THE WHITE BOX FOR NEW PRODUCT INNOVATION

breakfast was typically one of fatty meats with little if any fiber in the morning diet. This did not provide a good digestive start to the day. As interest in healthier foods was growing by the late 1800's, Henry D. Perky responded with his development of a machine to shred wheat and form it into bite size pieces. Later, the Kellogg brothers, one being a doctor, had experimented with various types of foods as served in a sanitarium. The patients liked the new food, and brought it home, sharing it with their families as the appeal grew. Through the years there were many new forms, tastes, and added ingredients that made this form of breakfast a big hit. What were the key factors that led to this innovation?

- Growth of employment away from home that drove a need for easier and faster ways to prepare a breakfast for people.

- Growing interest in healthier foods starting in the late 1800's.

- The insight that food grains provided better source of energy than the typical high fat breakfast of the time.

- Borrowing of new technology that was capable of cooking, flaking, puffing, and shredding various grains.

- Having the belief that food can be manufactured in large quantities for the masses.

Let's look at some more recent innovative new products and deconstruct the factors that might have led to their creation. In January 2014, Google® released news of its development of a contact lens that can monitor and measure a diabetic's glucose level in the tears of the eyes, and then signal the individual by a tiny flashing light in the contact lens when she needs to inject her insulin.

THE VISION DRIVING PROCESS - SEARCHING IN THE EXPANSION SPACE

Let's speculate on the possible pathways that could have arrived at this idea.

Here is one possibility:

- Observing the trend of rising health care costs which were driving greater interest and availability of medical self-diagnostic products.

- Google defined their business search to health care self-diagnostics.

- They further refined and defined their business in terms of diabetes care.

- Immersion in current state of the art medical care of diabetics.

- Decision to look at a component of diabetes care, glucose monitoring.

- Challenged existing beliefs that blood testing was the preferred or only potential marker for measuring glucose levels.

- Immersion in studying body fluids for glucose markers, and focusing on tears.

- Combining technologies, the contact lens, with new technology or miniaturized technology that converts glucose levels into electronic impulses.

- And, finally, by combining technologies, i.e. the electronic impulse with a tiny flashing light, Google was able to alert the individual in real time when the glucose level triggered an action, such as insulin injection or consumption of sweets.

SEARCHING OUTSIDE THE WHITE BOX FOR NEW PRODUCT INNOVATION

OR, another possibility:

- Google observed the trending towards greater consumer interest in acquisition of immediate real time data, eg GPS, Smartphones, text alerts, etc.

- Google defined their new business idea search into ways for consumers to access real time data by using their eyes.

- Then in a stroke of reversed mind thinking, Google made the leap to explore not what the eyes see, but rather, what we see in the eyes.

- Immersion into studies of the eyes and their chemistry to learn about what the chemistry says about our health.

- Discovery that the eye's tears contain glucose.

- Search of technologies that measure glucose levels.

- Combining technologies, i.e. contact lenses and electronics.

- And, finally, by combining technologies, i.e. the electronic impulse with a tiny flashing light, Google was able to alert the individual in real time when the glucose level triggered an action, such as insulin injection or consumption of sweets.

In another recent innovation, Nestle® is developing customized foods that can be made at home and catered to an individual's needs. In this new home counter top appliance, Nestle will be able to treat diseases with specialized foods for specific conditions. The foods will not be sold in stores, but rather, will be made available to the individual in their homes, with a machine that will tailor the food you eat to your malady. The process starts with an analysis of your condition and your

THE VISION DRIVING PROCESS - SEARCHING IN THE EXPANSION SPACE

so called nutrient profile. It will analyze the deficiencies and excesses in your diet, and then produce the right balance of nutrients, vitamins, minerals etc to cater to your needs. The machine would work like a coffee machine, but instead of processing coffee, it will process and deliver just the right balance of nutrients catered to you profile and condition, in either a liquid or powder form, ready to be taken or applied to your food on your plate.

So how did Nestle arrive at this innovation? The possible steps might have looked like this.

- Nestle decided to expand their business definition to include nutrients per se, separate from that which is delivered in traditional food by the products they market.

- They then took a further step in altering their business definition to expand from traditional methods of delivering nutrients to consumers via store bought food or supplement products. They asked " *how can we deliver nutrients right in the kitchen?* "

- Nestle observed several trends: a) That consumers were increasing their interest in healthy foods, and the desire to take more control of their health, b) That there was a growing trend towards customization and personalization, and c) Growing interest and use of counter top appliances that deliver food/beverage processing, such as single serve coffee makers, espresso machines, and counter top soda machines.

- Nestle immersed themselves in the current world of nutrition.

- They then challenged existing beliefs about how nutrition was delivered to consumers today via food or supplements. Are there better ways?

SEARCHING OUTSIDE THE WHITE BOX FOR NEW PRODUCT INNOVATION

- Nestle saw the existing world of blood work analyses for such things as cholesterol, sugar, and calcium levels as one part of a closed loop, and decided to close the loop with more immediate responsive action. This combination currently takes two steps, consumer knowledge, followed by consumer action in what they then bought and consumed. Nestle combined these two steps into one machine.

- In a very creative way, Nestle had the vision to think that what was done on a large scale in factories, ie manufacturing supplement pills, could be done on a small scale, and within the home. They borrowed and miniaturized the process, and took it out of the factory and brought it into the home.

From these few examples we can isolate and speculate on some of the mental touch points or stimuli that led to these innovations. If we conducted a more exhaustive study, it is likely that we would uncover more possible stimuli that helped drive innovations. Each innovation may have been driven by its own unique set of stimuli, whether by just one or two, or by a group of stimuli. While we can't know for sure which ones were the key factors, when we look at a range of innovations we can deduce that there are certain factors that we can speculate as the drivers. The most prevalent of these might include:

- The desire to satisfy one or more human needs.

- Personal conviction or mission.

- Clearly defined objective or business.

- Immersion in the prior knowledge within the arena.

- Awareness and application of trends.

THE VISION DRIVING PROCESS - SEARCHING IN THE EXPANSION SPACE

- A vision to see beyond the obvious of what was accepted.

- Challenging beliefs / what if's.

- Borrowing and / or combining behavior.

- Borrowing and / or combining technology.

- Mind Tools that force imaginative connections and new perspectives.

This deconstruction of historical innovations and the speculated mental steps that I have highlighted become the foundation for what I am presenting as the Vision Driving process. Our objective is to build on this foundation to create a prescribed pro-active process for generating NPD ideas to virtually any business arena in the hopes of creating a more robust front end funnel of NPD ideas, in quantity and quality.

CHAPTER 6

Vision Driving Essentials

In the previous chapter we deconstructed the possible pathways that led to the creation of a range of innovations to gain some insight into how they came to be. By building on these insights, we can formulate a prescribed process to assist us in stimulating the formation of new product ideas. That is where Vision Driving comes in.

Vision Driving is used to build a story about a need and a method of fulfillment, the two ends of the NPD idea that I talked about before. In this respect it differs greatly from the need-gap White Box approach which first identifies consumer needs, and then separately searches for the right need fulfillment, or technology. Vision Driving attempts to identify need and technology simultaneously. The objective is to optimize the need and the fulfillment with a technology or hypothesized technology. This doesn't mean that the referenced technology exists or that the technology application is feasible.

In the extreme case, it doesn't even mean that the technology can be created in our time, but by stretching our imagination in creating these new disruptive NPD ideas, the process can often times become the very driver for creating the new technology or application. Although there are exceptions, such as pure research projects which are pursued without foreknowledge or intent of specific applications,

VISION DRIVING ESSENTIALS

a project that pursues new technology applications would not be conducted without a reason. Whereas need-gap White Box analyses lead to NPD ideas that respond to unmet consumer needs within the known world of technology applications, Vision Driving does not suffer that limitation. Vision Driving is designed to create a reason for the technology or application, *before consumers ask for it.*

We can imagine that in a future world people do not have to clean their homes. It is done for them by self-cleaning robotic devices, large and small, some with our assistance and some without. If we can have timer controlled coffee makers, robotic pool cleaners, robotic welding machines in factories and robotic household floor cleaners, why can't we have timer controlled robotic cleaners to fully clean our homes while we go to work? In the future world of mobility we can press a button and be anywhere instantly. Letting go of the existing world and all its paradigms is but one Vision Driving method of stimulating new thinking that can lead us to disruptive ideas. Neither example may happen in our lifetime, but by thinking this way, we will stimulate new ideas that advance on present methods. And, simultaneously, such thinking will encourage the development and /or application of new technology.

As mentioned in the introduction, the power of Vision Driving is that it creates disruptive ideas, so don't look for mere linear extensions of the existing. Vision Driving provides a porthole to the future by stimulating our imagination. Are we ready for robotic cleaning sponges, or in-home on-demand fabricated custom fit garments, or electronic force field generated rain umbrellas, or Star Trek like teleportation devices (beam me up Scotty)?

One benefit of Vision Driving is somewhat akin to how science fiction has helped stimulate others to go on to create science fact. Vision Driving can provide the inspiration and motivation for creating new technologies.

SEARCHING OUTSIDE THE WHITE BOX FOR NEW PRODUCT INNOVATION

It was in the 1930's that Chester Gould introduced the world to the Dick Tracy® crime stopper cartoon character and his two way radio wrist watch. Call it science fiction or marketing fiction, but it was an idea ahead of its time. I am not sure if it was the inspiration for today's Smartwatches, but it surely laid out a vision for others to follow.

Who can forget Marty McFly and his hover board, the self levitating skate board minus the skates, as depicted in the 1989 movie *Back to the Future Part 2*? It may have seemed absurd then, but in 2015 a company named Hendo is introducing a hover board that levitates about 1 inch off the surface using a set of magnets and conductors. Who says that gravity isn't reversible? What was once fiction may now become reality.

Vision Driving is an iterative building process that can occur in a variety of settings. It can be the singular thought process of one individual working alone without any collaboration. It can be done in one's mind or on paper or both. It can be done as collaboration among a team of people, using any form of communication, not the least of importance is the easel pad or white board within a room setting. In any venue setting for Vision Driving, there are benefits to the iterative building process which allows time for incubation, collaboration, questions, answers, and progressive building of the ideas. Later I will describe how best to manage the Vision Driving process within a group setting.

The Vision Driving process is in some ways like several other mental process constructs that guide the thinker along a pathway from problem to solution. In the world of science the use of the scientific method is a prescribed process that is used to answer a particular problem or question. It starts with 1) an upfront statement of the problem or question, 2) extensive research on the subject, 3) preparation of an hypothesis, 4) experiments to support or refute the hypothesis, and finally, 5) conclusions.

Derivatives of the scientific method have been used in some fashion in other disciplines as well, not the least of which is business. The idea of a test market along with its action standards for success (the hypothesis) is a direct descendent of the scientific method. A test market is an experiment, and the use of controls in the test market is no different than those used in direct scientific studies.

In engineering, the thought process starts with a definition of the problem or stated objective, followed by research, technical speculations, possible solutions, applications, and testing. The final solution or application would then be selected based on its performance against the stated criteria.

In another engineering model for problem solving, the subject under study is mentally thermodynamically closed off and isolated by a set of fully encircling mental boundaries. The closed system is then studied by applying the law of conservation of mass and energy to guide the thinker to understanding what is happening inside the system.

And, when the subject is new product ideation, as is the case with Vision Driving, there are many precedents for using a prescribed process to lead us to new product ideas. The most often quoted term for creative problem solving and new product ideation, *Brainstorming*, is often used to describe any group setting where participants are assembled to think creatively about a stated objective or problem to solve. There are a variety of ways that the groups are conducted, but the essentials include: a moderator to guide the discussion, a set of prompts, props, questions, and other stimuli designed to encourage free flowing ideas, and a method of capturing ideas such as an easel pad. Brainstorming can be applied to just about any topic and is often used to generate a list of new product ideas.

Synectics is both a company and a method for creative problem solving. The method was invented by George M. Prince and William J.J.

Gordon, while working within the Arthur D. Little Invention Design Unit in the 1950s. The typical *Synectics* session will focus on one particular objective, problem, or area of interest. Through a series of stimuli, the moderator guides the team towards seeing a problem differently, and then using various mind tools such as analogies, the moderator provokes new perspectives on creative solutions. The process is more intense than Brainstorming, and more emotional, as the participants are asked to get more personally involved in a series of questions that spark their imaginations. *Synectics* is also more dependent on the skills of the moderator than in Brainstorming, as the process is more prescribed and deliberate in its attempt to force creative solutions that are not apparent.

Like these other prescriptions for problem solving, Vision Driving has its own set of steps designed to facilitate creative thinking. It is built on the observations of how historically disruptive new product ideas have been formulated, and then made more productive with a set of various stimuli. Vision Driving combines different types of stimuli to guide the creative process. Some stimuli are fully based in the real world (such as immersion in the business arena and trending analysis), while other stimuli may conjure up unfamiliar and/or abstract associations (such as challenging existing beliefs and mind tools).

The Vision Driving process provides a multitude of benefits in the search for NPD ideas:

1. It is designed to stretch our imagination in generating disruptive NPD ideas.

2. It is capable of stimulating a range of ideas to satisfy the need for a healthy volume of NPD ideas at the front end of the NPD Stage-Gate process.

3. The developed NPD ideas can create the descriptions of new technology and/or technology applications, *before the consumers ask for it.*

VISION DRIVING ESSENTIALS

4. The NPD ideas with their new technology or technology applications can become the basis for motivating the actual creation of the new technology that may not yet exist.

5. The NPD ideas may offer the business incentive for identifying derivative ideas that use more viable, do-able today technology, while still maintaining sufficient appeal and revenue potential.

First I offer a brief description of the whole Vision Driving process and then in subsequent chapters I drill down on each. Then, later in this book I offer examples of the Vision Driving process as applied to several arenas.

<u>The 8 Vision Drivers</u>

1. Clearly Defined Business and Objective.

2. Immersion in the Arena.

3. Trending Analysis, Observations and Applications.

4. Challenging Beliefs / What if's.

5. Borrowing and / or Combining Behavior.

6. Borrowing and / or Combining Technology.

7. Mind Tools that Stimulate the Imagination.

8. Idea Formation.

1. The very first step in this process is to **Define the Business** or need or activity that we want to explore for new products. How we define

this will have great bearing on how and what we explore. Very often a company may make the mistake early on by defining the business arena in a much too narrow way, and thus impose an initial limitation to what new ideas they may come up with. This may be done consciously or unconsciously. As described in *The Innovator's Dilemma*, many companies make the conscious decision to define their business as it exists today within a specified technology, and thereby set limitations early on to what they explore in NPD. The most often quoted example of this is when the railroads defined their business as railroads and not transportation, and thus did not see air travel as part of their business.

2. The next step is classic. Get to know your subject arena. **Immersion in the Arena** is vital to understanding the current behaviors, means and methods of need fulfillment, and attitudes. Much like the need-gap research, we look for grounding in the current range of needs, products, services that meet these needs. Immersion is important to a point. What we don't want to happen is an unconscious attachment to the current world approach to the business arena. To prevent this from happening, we will challenge everything we learn, as part of the 8 Vision Driving steps.

Once grounded in the business definition and a full immersion in the arena, we can move to the more stimulating steps in the Vision Driving process.

3. The merits of conducting **Trending Analysis** as we look at any business are well established. The logic here is that whatever our business arena, we operate in a larger world that is changing every day with implications to our business. If we can see these trends and understand their impact on our business, we can be better able to defend against a threat, or exploit an opportunity. In the Vision Driving process we want to look well beyond our own business arena in observing trends and then applying the insights to NPD ideation.

VISION DRIVING ESSENTIALS

4. When we **Challenge Beliefs** we are stopping the world for one instance and asking why. Why can't man fly? Can machines replicate the productive power of photosynthesis? Do we really believe that flies can self-generate from rotting flesh (spontaneous generation)? Is gravity reversible? If air pollution can harm us, is there anything we can place into our air that can improve our existence? (We do it with water by adding Fluoride into our water supply, why not with air?) The beauty of this exercise is that it forces us to revisit things in our everyday lives that we have never questioned before. And, it can be fun.

5 & 6. When we talk about **Borrowing or Combining Behavior and / or Technology** we are referring to a mental process that has literally created a world of change and new products. Innovation is a practice that borrows, combines, or builds on all known existing and prior technologies, innovations, insights, and discoveries. In the previous discussion we have seen how common this practice is and how it contributed to an endless list of innovations. This mental process is now a key step in the Vision Driving process.

The act of borrowing behavior is not as well studied as the act of borrowing technology. It is however, the more exciting tool for the very reason that it is less obvious. The Air Force has borrowed from nature (birds in flight) when it created the V formation of fighter jets. In packaging, the development of the clam shell comes directly from ….the clams. Placing a light on the front of the vacuum cleaner is borrowed from the use of hard hat lights used by coal miners. The simple suction cup designed to attach things to walls, comes from watching the animal world. And another borrow from the animal world is our use of sonar and radar borrowed from bats. As I discuss later, the borrowed behavior can come from the behavior of anything, living or not. This is an exciting and powerful Vision Driving tool.

7. **Mind Tools** have been described and discussed in many books and practices of creativity. They are meant to stimulate creativity, ask questions, suggest unfamiliar situations or perspectives, and establish a fun, imaginative environment. The classic tools include provocative suggestions like: make it very small, very large, look inside out, or upside down. Or try to separate the parts, reconfigure them, change their orientation, change their number, etc. Still other mind tools suggest changing your perspective (look outward from the item instead of looking inward), asking how nature would solve the task, or how a child would....and more.

8. The notion that **Idea Formation** is the final step in the process is actually a misnomer. Although it is shown as the logical final step, ideas are often formulated anywhere in the process. This is expected and should be encouraged. It is also expected that as the process continues, these earlier ideas can and should be built upon to create stronger ideas and / or derivative ideas.

As I explain throughout the rest of this book, and in particular with the actual Vision Driving application examples, it will become apparent that there are certain caveats to the process.

- Not all steps will be appropriate nor helpful in all ideation sessions, but you won't know it until you force it into the mental ideation process.

- NPD ideas can emerge from any single or multiple steps in the process, without going the full distance. Not all steps are always required to generate disruptive NPD ideas. Still, it is possible that good ideas developed in the early steps can be built up to even better ideas through the full 8 step process.

- Although the steps are shown as a progression, there is no reason not to loop back and forth, as ideas are built up.

VISION DRIVING ESSENTIALS

- The Vision Driving process can be applied over and over again for the same arena, generating different results.

- The time spent on the entire process as well as on each step will vary depending upon the business arena, the setting (i.e. team size and time clock constraints) and the task at hand. The need for homework and / or incubation time between steps can also affect the pace and timing of the entire Vision Driving Process.

CHAPTER 7

Defining the Business

If Google had not decided to expand their business definition to include new arenas, they would never have developed the glucose monitoring contact lens. But further in this thinking, if Google had decided to enter the blood glucose testing business instead of the self-diagnostics business (a much broader definition) it might not have arrived at a device that is placed in the eye. Instead, they may have pursued new technology for faster, easier blood glucose testing.

Years ago the Arm & Hammer ® Brand was known for its form of baking soda, or bicarbonate of soda, as used in baking to raise soda breads, fruit cakes, and other full flavored cakes. Their original business definition was probably described as a provider of ingredients for baking. But, as history shows, the management recognized that baking soda had a host of special properties that made it quite suitable for an ever expanding range of uses. Baking soda can absorb odors, remove some stains, and neutralize acid in the mouth, just to name a few. Today Arm & Hammer benefits from the vision of its management in expanding its business definition well beyond just a supplier of baking soda. In fact, their new business definition could be broadly defined as a provider of freshening and cleaning, which now includes a brand presence in multiple segments such as cleaning products, air fresheners, oral care products, and laundry detergents.

DEFINING THE BUSINESS

This brand stands as a perfect example of the benefits of an expanding and evolving business definition in building a brand and company.

How we define our business is vital to the overall strategic planning process. It tells us which business segment we are operating in, the life cycle of that business, who our competitors are, and our share position within that arena. Plus it has important consequences affecting every facet of the business, including the NPD programs.

In a sense, defining a business is a discretionary act by the marketer, but as I will explain, that doesn't mean that the world will agree. If we define our business too narrowly we may become threatened years hence by some seemingly unrelated business that encroaches and possibly marginalizes our own business. In simple terms, a decision to define your business in very narrow terms (i.e. by the current form, or product, or technology, or method of manufacture or distribution, etc) will lead your company towards very different strategies than if they define their business in broader terms. Meanwhile, other companies, whether within or outside your business arena may have a different perspective on how to build a business within your arena. If their business definition is not limited as your narrow definition, then we might see them enter the segment with a disruptive NPD entry that puts your business in a defensive mode. Again, the railroads as cited before, remain the most widely referenced example for those who chose to define their business narrowly by the current status quo, and lost out on emerging opportunities. Their business definition included the narrow description of trains and not the broader description of transportation.

Narrow business definitions that include specific reference to product forms or technologies will place particular limitations on that company's growth trajectory. The mistake could be twofold: 1) we would be less likely to look for alternative forms or new technologies to replace our chosen form, and at the same time, 2) we would never see the threat from others who are doing that looking. If a company wants to stay ahead of the competitive change curve, then the search for new forms and technologies should be unlimited, inside or outside the arena. Unless a company looks beyond their arena, they will never see the emerging technology threats and opportunities coming.

One of the most obvious examples in recent times of the pitfalls and benefits of business definitions is in book selling. Two companies had two different business definitions, one a narrow view, and the other a broader view, in this case about how the product or service was "delivered" to the consumer. Booksellers like Borders defined their business as retail stores that sell books, and music, and other materials. As the world changed, with new technologies and trends creating changes in the way we access these materials, opportunities and threats emerged for the likes of Borders. But, Borders was stuck in its business definition as a bricks and mortar retailer. It could not, or did not want to recognize the changing world where such materials could be accessed via on-line sales with door to door delivery, or via electronic transfer to tablets, such as e-readers. Borders went out of business and filed for bankruptcy in 2011 because it did not evolve its business definition to a changing world.

On the other hand, Amazon® chose to define their business based on a broader idea involving *access* to consumer goods. Their definition changed the existing paradigm: *from* the idea that *access* meant walking into a store to purchase an item, *to* a different idea of *access* involving opening your door and bending down at your doorstep to acquire an item. This change in definition has become more appealing to consumers as evident by the huge success of Amazon. And, by the way, it should be apparent to anyone paying attention that Amazon continues to evolve its business definition in seeking growth opportunities well beyond "easy access to books".

DEFINING THE BUSINESS

Another somewhat similar example is the demise of Blockbuster® movie rentals, who viewed their business as limited to offering walk in physical acquisition of movie DVDs. They did not pursue the broader business definition of "....making movies available to consumers.... by *whatever means*..." Blockbuster might have seen the emerging technology that would make this viable, but they did not react appropriately, nor fast enough. Netflix® did this, and indeed marginalized the viability of Blockbuster.

The way we define our business has particular importance to the Vision Driving process since it also defines the scope of our NPD focus within a defined business arena. The process can be applied to any business definition or any business arena to generate NPD ideas. However, the process is more likely to generate disruptive NPD ideas when the business definition represents some expansion, in any of the elements, from the current. If the goal is disruption, consider an expansion of your business definition.

Question: Are manufacturers of skin sun protective products in the sun protection business, or the skin care business, or in the OTC Drug skin protection business, or the cosmetic skin business? Each definition will lead to different places in the NPD ideation process. If we are in the OTC Drug skin sun protection business then we will never contemplate non-OTC Drug means of protection whether they are fabrics, or clothing, or personal sun umbrellas, or electronic devices. With a narrow business definition that focuses exclusively on OTC Drugs, we would never pursue devices like our idea for an electronic magic wand that creates some new means to protect skin from the sun. Defining our business is our decision and our discretion about the scope, the nature, and the direction of our business growth.

Even if you are defining your business as OTC Drugs for skin sun protection you had better become aware of any and all alternative means of protection that circumvent OTC Drugs. Just because you limit your

◄ SEARCHING OUTSIDE THE WHITE BOX FOR NEW PRODUCT INNOVATION

business definition doesn't mean the world will limit its pursuit to that definition. While I am not aware of any such technology today, someday we could have the hand held electronic wand device that "showers" the body with electronic ions that protect the skin from the sun's damaging rays. It's clearly not an OTC Drug, but it gets the job done, and without messy lotions. It encroaches on the OTC Drug alternatives and can marginalize your business.

Another new idea for instance, a hand held device that uses a set of sensors and software algorithms to calculate the intensity of the sun's rays and the time spent in the sun to then alert the sunbather to unhealthy levels of sun exposure, would also not be pursued by your company. First, it's a device and not an OTC Drug, and second, it offers a different form of protection, ie *it offers information* that protects the individual. If instead you define your business more broadly than OTC Drugs, to skin sun protection, *by whatever means*, you would be open to these new technologies for your business, and might even lead the way.

Given the importance of the business definition for our company, we must first agree on the elements of a business definition, before we go into any evaluation mode. Once our definition includes all the key elements we can then go on to judge if that definition is right for the company and our growth objectives.

Any business is defined by certain key elements which will create the framework for the business as it exists today, and where it wants to grow in the future.

1. What needs do we satisfy?

2. What product or service do we provide?

3. Who are our primary consumers or customers?

DEFINING THE BUSINESS

4. How shall we provide/distribute our product or service to them?

5. How shall we configure our service or manufacture our product?

When we build our business definition, we should notice that the subtlety of our chosen responses to the elements will have a significant effect on how we conduct our business and where we will look for growth.

Referring to our discussion about the skin care company, the business managers would face a range of business definition options. In these few examples shown below, we alter just the first line of each definition relating to the 1st and 2nd elements in the business definition (Need satisfied + Product provided), to highlight how just one set of variables can have a dramatic impact on the business.

A. We market **OTC Drug skin protection products** to all consumers...

B. We market **any/all types of skin protection products** to all consumers...

C. We market **OTC Drug skin sun protection products** to all consumers....

D. We market **any/all types of skin sun protection products** to all consumers...

E. We market **skin sun protection umbrellas** to all consumers...

F. We market **skin sun protection hats** to all consumers...

◄ SEARCHING OUTSIDE THE WHITE BOX FOR NEW PRODUCT INNOVATION

G. We market **all types of skin sun protection garments** to all consumers...

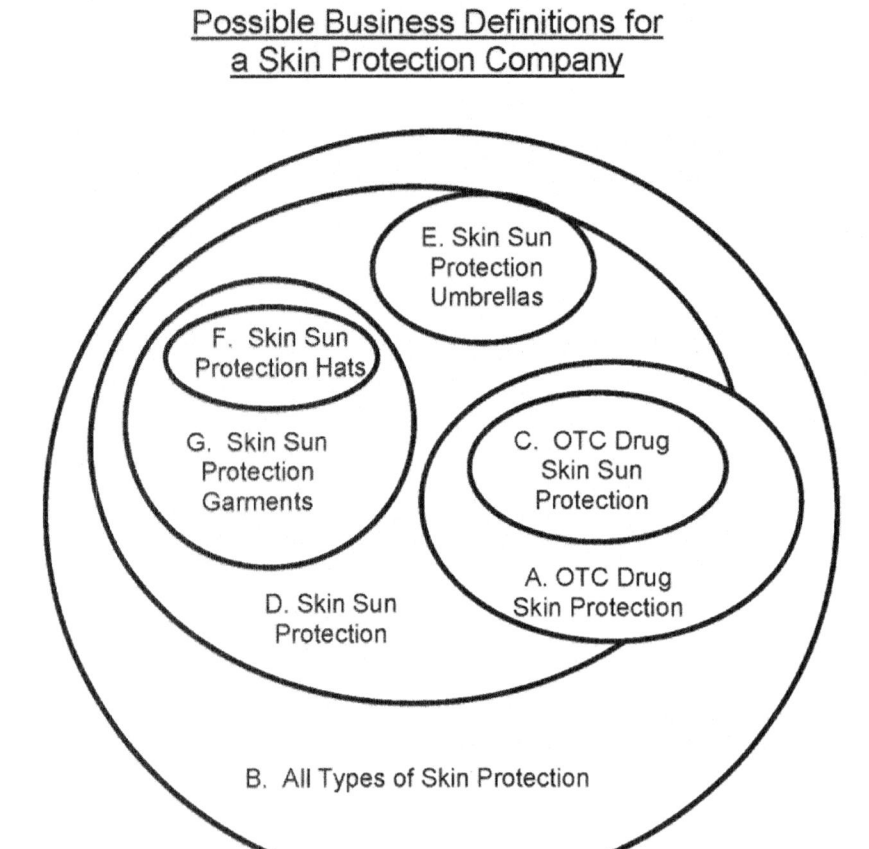

Possible Business Definitions for a Skin Protection Company

- E. Skin Sun Protection Umbrellas
- F. Skin Sun Protection Hats
- G. Skin Sun Protection Garments
- C. OTC Drug Skin Sun Protection
- A. OTC Drug Skin Protection
- D. Skin Sun Protection
- B. All Types of Skin Protection

In these few examples we altered just two elements of the business definition to highlight how a difference in just a few words can have significant implications on what we do as a business. As we look at this diagram we can see how each business definition puts us in a different place within the strategic arena of *All Types of Skin Protection*.

We could conduct the same exercise for the other three elements of the business definition to help us look at the larger strategic picture.

◄ 86

DEFINING THE BUSINESS

As we think about the mathematical permutations of altering each of the elements, it is easy to see that there can be dozens of options in any business definition.

In two common examples, Amazon and Netflix, each altered the traditional business definition of their key competitors regarding two other elements

4. How shall we provide/distribute our product or service to them?

5. How shall we configure our service or manufacture our product?

Both companies changed the paradigms within their business segments, and achieved great success by modifying their business definitions in how products were configured and delivered to their customers.

All companies need to re-visit the business definition for each of their operating segments annually as the pace of events, competitive activities, behavioral changes, technology, and other trends are only accelerating. As these changes occur, there are always emerging opportunities for doing things differently, for satisfying needs differently, for changing people's expectations, and so forth. Likewise, any of these changes can threaten your business in ways that might ultimately marginalize your methods, products, services, etc.

I view this dynamic as a corollary to the thinking in *Chaos Theory*, and in particular by what is called *The Butterfly Effect*, as coined by Edward Lorenz. The thinking goes that a small change in air currents that happens when a butterfly flaps its wings will in some way alter larger, far away, and possibly much later climatic conditions. In this context it would behoove a company to keep its eyes on all

SEARCHING OUTSIDE THE WHITE BOX FOR NEW PRODUCT INNOVATION

"butterfly activities" so to speak, as they review their business definition and strategies. Clearly this is not an easy task. It takes a team that is constantly reviewing the world of activities well beyond their particular business. As butterflies are noticed you must always be asking: How does this affect my business paradigm? How must we alter our business, and/or prepare the business to meet the threats and opportunities that are emerging?

Although Kodak® was actually the first to invent digital photography, they were extremely uncomfortable about giving up their dominant role in film based photography. They were so heavily invested in the film paradigm that they just could not let go. And, part of their dilemma was that they were unable or unwilling to devise a viable business model in digital photography that could replace their current profit stream. As they sat and talked, Kodak also watched as others exploited the new technology and advanced their own successful business models. Noticing changes, as difficult as it is by itself, is not nearly as difficult as integrating those changes into your business definition and model. This is one of the stated pitfalls of the *Innovator's Dilemma*. It often takes courage, ingenuity, and great internal salesmanship to convince management to change course, however small or big.

Unfortunately, as in many human activities, reaction in business can sometimes be a lot easier than pro-action. It is the great companies that both notice the changes and exploit them pro-actively, by continually evolving their business definitions as necessary to stay competitive and vital. Some of the best examples of companies that continually re-visit, revise, and expand their business definitions include Google, Nike, Amazon, Apple, and P&G. It is no coincidence that such companies continue to grow.

So, how do we select the best business definition for our company? By what set of objectives and criteria do we choose the optimal definition? Bingo. That is the question.

DEFINING THE BUSINESS

First, start with your current business definition by assigning statements to each of the five elements. Who are you today? What needs do you satisfy? What product or services do you provide? How? And so forth. Then examine each element and ask who your competitors are, and how they define their business. Then, you must pressure test each element by asking what the alternatives might look like and what their implications might be. This exercise in itself can be an eye opener.

When pressure testing for alternatives, you must look well beyond your focused arena. Ask how changing events are impacting your arena, or how they might in the future. There are truly no limits to what you look at.

Although the focus of this book is predominantly on the first two elements to the business definition (1. What needs do we satisfy? and 2. What product or service do we provide?), your review and pressure testing of the business definition should include all five elements. You won't know if there are disruptive ideas waiting for your business in these elements, unless you ask the questions.....just as Amazon did.

At this point, you have arrived at an initial draft of your business definition as it is today along with the possible set of alternatives. Then comes the tough part. How do you react to what you see? Again the key questions are: how do we select the best business definition for our company? By what set of objectives and criteria do we choose?

Much of the answers depend on your company's assets, strengths, growth objectives, and courage. Those are serious considerations. Kodak saw the emergence of digital photography but fell into the trap of trying to protect their immediate assets and strengths vs. pursuing a plan to evolve and grow into the changes. They did not have the courage or creativity to make the change.

◄ **SEARCHING OUTSIDE THE WHITE BOX FOR NEW PRODUCT INNOVATION**

Your business must make decisions today for tomorrow. If after inputting the results of your analysis, you decide to stay with your current business definition, then that is a conscious informed decision. Perhaps the search revealed no apparent need to alter your definition, or perhaps the cited emerging changes are seen as far away. It may be that your company does not want to take risks outside its current comfort zone. Or perhaps your company has decided that they would rather build up their position in the current arena as a conscious business decision, and then later, perhaps, set out to acquire any emerging company that is successfully exploiting changes. Or, perhaps your company has decided that within their larger product portfolio there were other segments that offered more promising growth trajectories. For whatever the reason, if your company consciously stays with its current business definition, it must also consciously accept the possible consequences: 1) missed opportunities, 2) future threats from others, and in the worst case scenario, 3) become obsolete and be put out of business.

The business that is currently marketing OTC Drug skin protection products would someday face a dilemma if they did not look at other emerging technologies that could replace OTC Drug products with electronic or other methods of skin protection. *The Butterfly Effect* as I referred to is something to bear in mind. The companies that are always looking well beyond their business arena will be first to recognize the changes and be able to see how to exploit them, whether by altering their business definition, or by acquiring new brands and/or companies.

From the Greek philosophers we are told to *Know Thyself First*. Meaning: before you can fully understand others and take guidance from what you see around you, you must first be honest with yourself. In business this would translate to a soul searching discussion of your assets, strengths, weaknesses, goals, and courage, before you can determine the best course of action for the business. You can't start to make changes, or exploit the changes around you, unless you know where you are starting from and where you want to go.

So, back to our earlier questions: How do we select the best business definition for our company? By what set of objectives and criteria do we choose?

The answer is: we ultimately make the decision based on our own soul searching review of who we are, how much we want to grow, where and how we want to grow, and what strengths and resources we could bring to bear to support that growth. We would also take measure of our fortitude in leveraging those strengths, and our comfort level for taking on risk. And, as we conduct this review and make our decisions, we would be weighing the risk of staying with a current business definition vs the risk of attempting change.

Whatever decisions we make through this exercise, we will at least have become aware of the larger strategic arena that we operate in, and we would become more mindful of the potential for future threats and opportunities.

If your company's objective is to secure or maintain a competitive advantage or leadership role, or to expand and grow aggressively, then it may be well served to expand its current business definition. Doing so will also provide more fertile ground for pursuing disruptive NPD programs which can support those aggressive growth objectives.

CHAPTER 8

Immersion in the Arena

The traditional importance of an a priori immersion in the business arena is likewise important to the Vision Driving process. Whatever our business, we must know the environment, the competitive landscape, the consumer behavior, current technology, government regulations, and other factors that affect the business. Every good marketer should be grounded in these factors and any changes that emerge, year to year. For the Vision Driving process it is a necessary step.

Since this step is well established in all marketing practices, there is not much more to add. The immersion should include a review of all available secondary data, including retail data, consumer behavior, competitive dynamics, technology, regulatory environment, and just about any insight or data that relates to the subject arena.

If the arena in review is a business that satisfies human health issues, then it helps to fully understand the physiologies of the human anatomy involved. If the arena is focused on transportation, or the weather, or a manufacturing process, or whatever, then we must know as much as possible about that dynamic.

As it is becoming clear in this book, my philosophy is that any business segment immersion should go well beyond the arena in terms of trends, technologies, behaviors, etc. Much of this extended immersion will reveal itself by the Vision Driving steps which are intended to force our sights well beyond any particular segment under review.

Sometimes primary research is necessary. This is where the world of marketing research lives. There is no end to what market researchers will suggest, so this is where real judgment pays off. There is *need to know* and *nice to know* research. Make sure you pursue what is absolutely necessary and not any more. Research can be important. But, as fully detailed in earlier chapters, this type of research should not be used as the *exclusive* basis for NPD ideation through the unearthing of need-gap White Space or White Box opportunities. Immersion research is a start in the NPD ideation process, not the end.

One of the insights to be gained from an immersion exercise is a determination of the maturity of the segment. Is it embryonic, rapid growth, growth, mature, or declining? As discussed in a prior chapter, this determination has important bearing on the type of NPD strategies that a company may pursue, whether the company is already a player in the business, or contemplating becoming one.

CHAPTER 9

Trending Analysis - Observation Tools

The role of trends in driving innovation is greater today than ever before. This is a direct result of our advances in communication and travel. It is hard to imagine a trend developing and extending without lines of communication. Trends are like sound waves. Sounds don't exist in the voids of space. They need to travel in a medium to exist, whether in a gas like air, or liquid like oceans, or any solids. Like sound, trends cannot exist in a vacuum. They need to be observed and communicated via voice, travel, print communications, electronic, audio or visual communications, and any other means. If a trend cannot extend itself then it cannot have impact. Early man and early man's innovations were slower in coming and less driven by trends, because the lines of communication were primitive. As mankind created advancements in communication and travel technologies, the occurrence and impact of trends have become increasingly more apparent. Today, trends can literally travel at the speed of light.

In our previous chapters we had deconstructed various historical innovations and have seen that trending may have been a factor in driving some of the more recent creations. Looking at the world today, we see many innovations, products and services, where trends may have been a driving factor. Some examples:

TRENDING ANALYSIS - OBSERVATION TOOLS

- The Green Energy movement has clearly given rise to a range of new products and services, including the push for electric and hybrid cars.

- The increasingly hostile world from man-made and natural disasters has spawned the growth in new survival aids, personalized power sources, long lasting food supplies, and other items for emergency preparedness.

- More seniors living alone and living longer has driven the rise of various products and services to assist these folks in their safety and medical needs, including wearable alert callers, and home visiting elder care services.

- Increased threats from computer hacking and identify fraud has driven the growth of new identify theft protection services.

- Two trends, the growing use of Smartphones for photography and the continued growth of clanning and sharing have driven the emergence and growth of photo sharing services such as Shutterfly® and Snapfish®, etc.

- With the rise in children's abductions and school shootings, as well as the introduction of GPS tracking apps, we see the growth of a new sub-segment in child safety, ie the use of GPS tracking wearables for kids.

- The growing concern for the spread of germs has led to the emergence of hand sanitizer stations in public places, including the entrance to various retail stores.

- The growing use of smart technologies plus the trend towards home energy management has led to the increased appeal of proximity sensors in home interiors that activate lights only when someone is in the room.

SEARCHING OUTSIDE THE WHITE BOX FOR NEW PRODUCT INNOVATION

The more recent the innovation, the more likely that trending of some type played a role in stimulating its formation. This would parallel the advancements in communication and travel. Within the Vision Driving process we seize upon this insight and make trending analysis an explicit stimulus in creating NPD ideas in the Expansion Space

In the past 50 years or so, the study of trends has become more accepted and prevalent. There are many notable trending analysts who offer their insights into trends and how they will impact our lives and businesses. The big trends are often stated and restated by these "authorities". At the very least, smart marketers already know that by aligning their initiatives or new products to the macro trends they can create more appealing and successful programs. We all know about the big trends such as rising health care costs, climate change, people working later in life, more 24/7 services, etc. In day to day marketing it is up to us to factor these into our plans.

Within Vision Driving we go beyond this notion of trend alignment to our business plans. In both the **Method of Observation** and in the **Method of Application**, trending analysis becomes a more integral part of the Vision Driving ideation process.

First, in regard to the **Method of Observation**, instead of relying on outside experts to share their findings, the Vision Driving process forces the ideator to take charge of the observations herself. In Vision Driving, we first give the ideator the **Observation Tools** to conduct her own trending analysis. This has multiple benefits:

1. It empowers the ideator to become more observant of the world around her, and makes this a part of her everyday marketing function. She will become a better marketer and better able to create disruptive ideas.

TRENDING ANALYSIS - OBSERVATION TOOLS

2. It forces the unearthing of deeper, more nuanced trends, well beyond the macro trends that are often quoted by these "experts". This ensures that this ideator has the opportunity to generate more insightful thinking beyond the oft quoted trending insights that are available to all her competitors.

3. It will save the cost of bringing in the same experts that are sharing the same data with your competition.

Next, in the **Method of Application**, the Vision Driving process teaches the ideator the **Application Tools** to apply these trend observations towards the creation of more disruptive products in the Expansion Space.

In this chapter we focus on the **Observation Tools.**

The world changes every day, with events creating threats and opportunities for individuals, companies, and countries. Sole events are occurring all the time, in all facets of human and non-human activities, and they are occurring everywhere. In small ways or big ways each event can have an impact, whether it is close by or far away geographically or conceptually. With today's fast and widespread means of communications, these impacts can literally occur at the speed of light.

When a hurricane like Sandy occurs it is no doubt an event, having an impact on our lives generating both threats and opportunities. Singular events like this occur all the time in all facets of our human experience.

EVENT
Hurricane Sandy

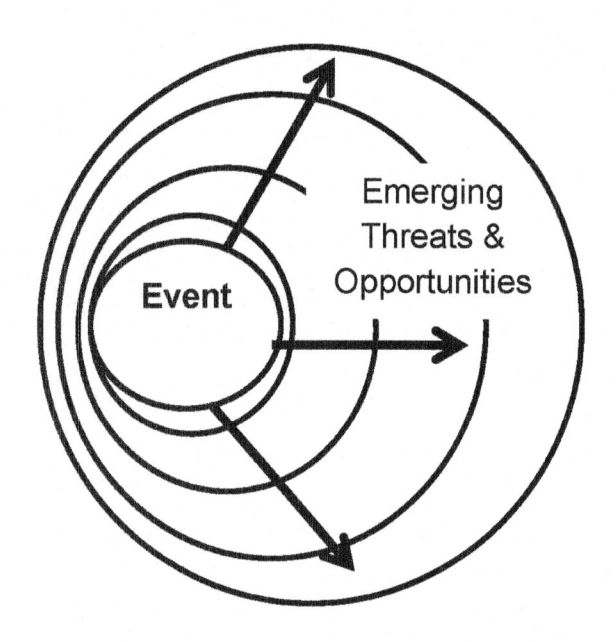

When the event occurs with more frequency, and/or in more locations, and over an extended period of time, like an increase in the frequency of extreme weather droughts, hurricanes, tornadoes, etc it can be called a Trend.

TRENDING ANALYSIS - OBSERVATION TOOLS ➤

TREND
Climate Change

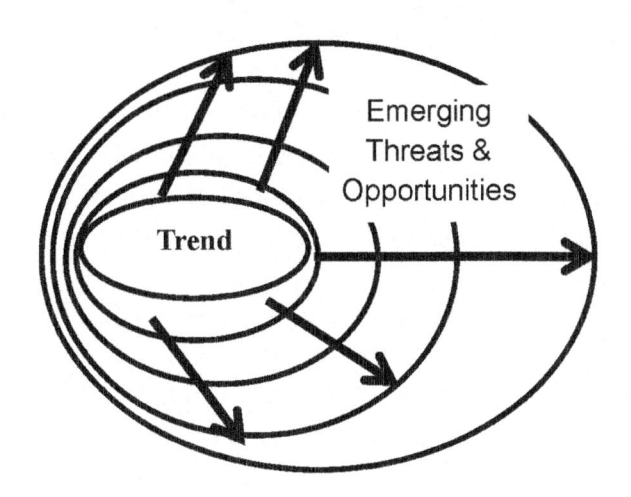

[Diagram: concentric ellipses labeled "Trend" at center with arrows radiating outward to "Emerging Threats & Opportunities"]

There are obvious sources of trending information like TV, newspapers, internet, Trade Shows, Patent Gazette, Trade and Professional publications, suppliers, etc. Many companies focus on a handful of sources like these within their own industry as a way to stay current in their business and as a possible way to find NPD ideas. This is fine, but is a grossly inadequate view of the larger picture of a changing world.

When we speak about the **Observation Tools** for the ideator the first task is to recognize that the data sources are all around us. From the moment we awake to the moment we fall asleep we are confronted with a barrage of information, in words, visuals, and sounds that reveal a changing environment. The information is all around us. We have to learn to see it, absorb it, and question it so we can identify emerging trends.

Our goal is to see more and see it first before our competitors do. We must sharpen our **Observation Tools** so that they are an integral

SEARCHING OUTSIDE THE WHITE BOX FOR NEW PRODUCT INNOVATION

part of our day to day lives. If we spend our time looking down at a Smartphone, we will never see the changing world around us. We must notice everything, ask questions, and be able to make connections. If we look up from the streets of some big cities, we would notice the increased presence of not only surveillance video cameras but more recently, we would see multi-sensor devices that can measure movement, temperature, noise levels, pollution, and more. There is a trend here. What does this mean for our privacy, our safety, for local merchant marketing, for real estate values, etc?

When we see new retail stores opening in our neighborhood, or others that are closing, we may be seeing a trend. Why are there more nail salons, dollar stores, and emergency medical services, while fewer shoe repair shops and dedicated retail floral shops? We may also learn from noticing which new magazines emerge, and which ones die off. What does it mean when we see more and more sharing dynamics, whether photo sharing via the internet, or automobile or bicycle sharing in the real world? Why are we seeing a growth in red-light cameras at road intersections?

Observing and deciphering events and trends can be exciting, challenging, and very rewarding. Events and trends have signals, and the sources can be found everywhere around us. Every day these signals are there for those of us who have learned to see and hear them.

TRENDING ANALYSIS - OBSERVATION TOOLS

Sources of Event and Trend Signals

Sources feeding into an **Observed Event**:
- News
- Magazines
- Retail Sales
- Store Checks
- Trade Shows
- Trade Publications
- Consumer Behavior
- Advertising
- TV Shows
- Technology Publications
- Competitive Practices
- Best Practices
- New Products
- Government Actions
- Research
- Personal Experiences

Once we have noticed an event, we must then ask some questions. *Is this just a one-off event or a series of connected events? Is it a trend? Why is this happening? What is driving this? What are the factors that make this possible?* When we ask these questions we are forcing our scrutiny that will uncover the factors creating the trend, their connections to each other, and the implications, narrow and broad. By deeply studying each event occurrence, we can uncover insights that others may be missing. That is the power of this process and as a Vision Driving tool.

Sources of Event and Trend Signals

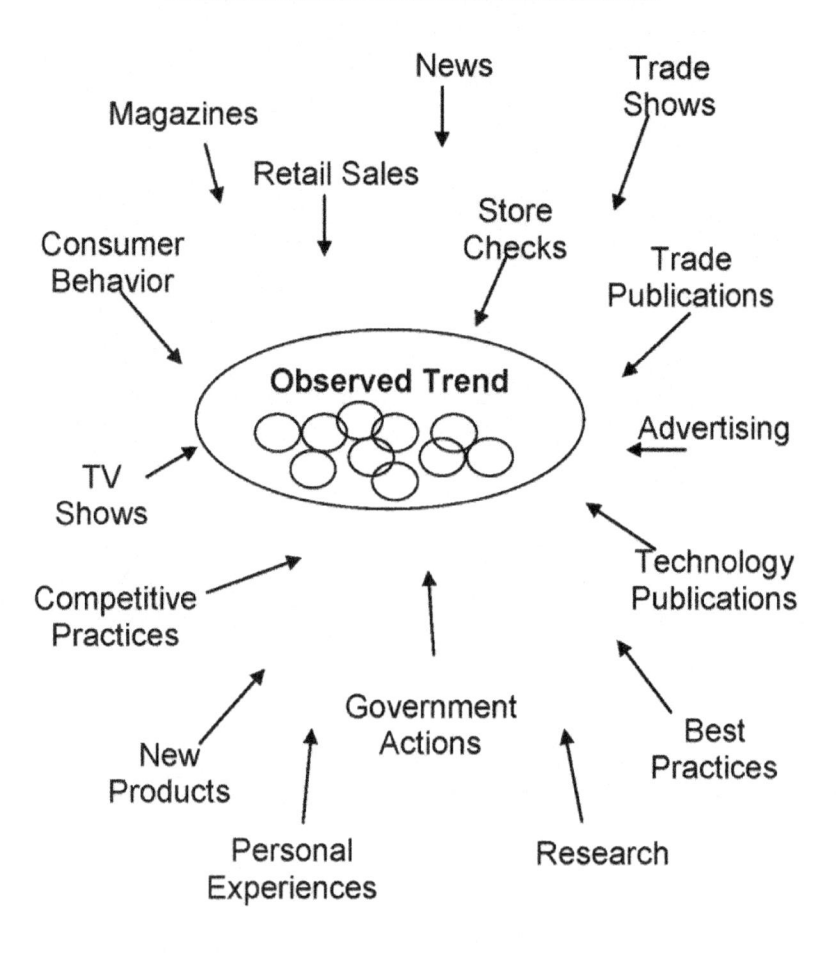

- News
- Magazines
- Trade Shows
- Retail Sales
- Store Checks
- Consumer Behavior
- Trade Publications
- **Observed Trend**
- Advertising
- TV Shows
- Technology Publications
- Competitive Practices
- New Products
- Government Actions
- Best Practices
- Personal Experiences
- Research

TRENDING ANALYSIS - OBSERVATION TOOLS

Observed Trend Example

```
        Magazines    News       Trade Shows
                      ↓
                  Retail Sales
                      ↓
   Consumer        Store Checks      Trade
   Behavior            ↓          Publications
           ↘   ┌─────────────────┐  ↙
               │  Observed Trend │
               │ Growing Appeal of│  ← Advertising
    TV    →    │Natural Ingredients│
   Shows       └─────────────────┘
                       ↑              ↖ Technology
   Competitive                          Publications
   Practices         ↑
        ↗                          ↖
    New        Government            Best
   Products    Actions             Practices
       ↑           ↑                  ↑
                                 Research
               Personal
              Experience
```

One example of a trend that is right in front of us is the emergence of TV monitors in public spaces. This may not be a significant trend but it is a perfect example to demonstrate the **Observation Tools.** We first began to see TVs in bars, and then their descendants, sports bars. Then a few years ago we saw them emerge in airports, and more recently we see them in lobbies of hotels, banks, office buildings, as well as in doctor's offices, public rest areas, etc. First question, Is *this a trend?* As we see the growing use of public displayed TV monitors, and see this spreading to new public space environments, we would have to say yes, it is a trend.

Next, *Why is this occurring?* We notice that in the first grouping of bars and sports bars these TVs have their basis in entertainment (and profit motive for the owner of the bar), while in the latter groups, the more recent groups, the basis for their presence is in something else.

If we sharpen our **Observation Tools**, and ask penetrating questions, we can see that this is a trend with several factors at play. So why are we seeing more TVs in public spaces?

- The emergence of new wide flat screen TVs has made the placement of TVs more efficient in their use of space.

- These wider screens have facilitated a larger viewing distance as for larger spaces.

- Growing 24/7 news content has created a more widespread universally appealing content for the general population.

- Sadly, more and more of today's events are about human violence and tragedies that generate tremendous and immediate interest by the public.

- Specific groups of people have become more acutely interested in the daily news where it might affect them directly and immediately, as when a traveler might be affected by a snow storm in her route, or a working mom may need to know if her child is safe after a school shooting.

When we ask penetration questions as to why this is occurring, we can see the basis for the trend reveal itself. As shown above, this particular trend is based on the convergence of improved technology,

TRENDING ANALYSIS - OBSERVATION TOOLS

an increasingly more dangerous world, more available 24/7 content, and changes in consumer attitudes and behavior.

When looking at all the kinds of trends that are occurring, it helps to collect our observations and place them into clusters or groupings. This is a useful technique that helps us in the Vision Driving process to see patterns of trends as well as to provide more precise stimulation in the ideation process.

There are a variety of types of trends, some relating to technology, some to consumer behavior, some involving the environment, the government, and so forth. I find it useful to cluster these into 4 types of trends:

- **Marketplace:** Media / Competition / Retailing

   What is happening in the business world around us?
   What kind of trends do we see in advertising media?
   Are there changes in the way companies are doing business?
   How do consumers research products, order, and acquire products?

- **Consumer:** Behavioral / Demographic / Societal

   How is behavior changing, attitudes, relationships, and values?
   What are the changing work patterns?
   What changes do we see in family structure?

- **Macro-Economic:** Industrial / Regulatory / Environmental

   How are government regulations affecting our lives?
   What trends do we see in climate, weather, and pollution?
   What changes are taking place in manufacturing?

◄ SEARCHING OUTSIDE THE WHITE BOX FOR NEW PRODUCT INNOVATION

- **Technology Trending**: Inside & outside our arena

What emerging technologies have more widespread applications?
Which technologies are receiving the greatest attention?
Which technologies are crossing over into other areas?

The identification of trends is a continuous process since by its nature new trends emerge every day as the world changes around us. Every day brings us new observations to study, and every day we face the same questions about whether or not the event is part of a trend. Here we list just a few of these trends as of this writing, to be used as examples for describing how this fits within the Vision Driving process. This list of trends and their descriptions will continue to change and expand as we observe and analyze the dynamic changes in the world around us.

When first looking at trending as part of the Vision Drivers, we are not concerned about the relationship or impact of the trend on the arena in study, not yet anyway. At this point, we are observing the world and trying to make connections between events to determine if there is a trend occurring. If we do our homework correctly, we will begin to see the world in a more dynamic way, with its many layers and currents of movements. In the next chapter we study those movements and seek to understand how they drive general opportunities. Finally, within the Vision Driving exercise we will re-visit all such trending observations and general opportunities and ask how they might drive the creation of specific new NPD ideas in our business arena.

But first, we start with the listing of some of these observed trends.

TRENDING ANALYSIS - OBSERVATION TOOLS

Marketplace: Media / Competition / Retail

TRENDS
Growing appeal and use of on-line retailing; Retailers losing relevance; Showrooming
Need for more accessible and low cost medical services;   Drug Chains offering more walk in medical services
Growth of non-charge card payments such as Apple® Pay
More organic products availability, more retail competition for Whole Foods®
Growth of robot service assistants in retail (Lowes®)
More media types in more places, both public and personal, and more interaction between them
More advertising dollars moving from traditional media to "new media" such as social media, mobile, web, etc.
More personalized / customized products & services
More immediate availability of items purchased on line eg Amazon® same day delivery, FreshDirect® food delivery
Mobil apps and connectivity between smart phones and retail transactions
Growing 24/7 working class & lifestyles

Consumer: Behavioral / Demographic / Societal

TRENDS
Changing " face " of retirement; more part time retirement, more retired population, more retirees free time
Half of all meals are now eaten alone (but many with TV, iPad®, Smartphone, newspaper, etc)
More single households
Increased clanning and sharing via texting, skyping, Facebook® and photo sharing such as Snapfish®, Shutterfly®, etc
Increased use of specialized / customized virtual communities: singles like match.com® , home owners like Angie's list ®), political candidates, political and health causes, etc
Increased concerns for spread of diseases and food contaminations
As cost of living increases, consumers show continued interest in small low cost indulgences

TRENDING ANALYSIS - OBSERVATION TOOLS

Consumer: Behavioral / Demographic / Societal

TRENDS
Growing interest in electric cars
Less time spent in home cooking, Increased food consumption out of home
Use of shared transportation, ie car sharing and bike sharing: Car2Go®, Zipcar®, Citibike®, etc
Use of public surveillance cameras of people behavior
Interest in healthy nutrition, organic foods
Cashless transactions; Consumers carrying less cash (Apple Pay®)
Growth of Hispanics
Growing 24/7 working class & lifestyles

Macro-Economic:
Industrial / Regulatory / Environmental

TRENDS
Rising health care costs
Inner cities reaching limits on congestion
More disruptive weather
Continued reduction in the ozone layer
More government intervention & controls
Increased threats from cyber hacking of companies, retailers, etc
Greater controls on greenhouse gases
Use of RFID wireless tracking devices
Rising taxes
Growth of solar panel use
More use of public surveillance cameras
More hostile world coming closer to home

TRENDING ANALYSIS - OBSERVATION TOOLS

Technology Trending: Inside & outside our arena

TRENDS
Growing use of portable devices
Video Training
Growing use of public / environmental data gathering by multi-sensor surveillance (e.g. people movements, sound, temperatures, air quality, etc)
Growing use of Skype ™ and Google Plus®
Emerging technology for social robots
Growing use of Smartphones for medical condition sensors and self diagnosis, plus virtual contact with Physicians
Growth of renewable energy sources and consumption: like wind, solar, wave, hydroelectric
Increased applications for 3-D printing
Connectivity: people to people, people to things, things to things
Incorporating "smart technology" into traditional appliances, into home management, transportation, etc.

◄ SEARCHING OUTSIDE THE WHITE BOX FOR NEW PRODUCT INNOVATION

Technology Trending: Inside & outside our arena

TRENDS
Wearable technology (eg Google® Glass, and Smartwatches)
Portable power sources Longer battery life
Medical implants and miniature digestible sensors and imaging
Growing use of drones for business in delivery and aerial observations
Growing use of Cloud storage
Growth of Big Data
GPS applications
Nanotechnology

We observe and analyze trends because they have impact on our businesses. They cause opportunities and threats, at the same time, but for different groups. In the Vision Driving process our goal is to first identify the trends, then apply these findings towards a statement of potential general opportunities, and finally, to apply those insights towards the specific arena in review in creating new disruptive NPD ideas.

The second set of tools for trending analysis provide the ideator or team with the **Application Tools,** as discussed in the next chapter.

CHAPTER **10**

Trending Analysis - Application Tools

The use of trending analysis as a factor in NPD idea formation is not new. One of the great trend watchers and a self-described Futurist, *Faith Popcorn*, wrote about the importance of using trend analysis as one measure of a new product's potential for success. In her book *Clicking*, Popcorn posits that the best new ideas are those that touch on at least 3 trends. If it does, then the idea *Clicks!* , as she called it. She maintains that if a new idea does not meet this threshold, then it will not be aligned with the emerging opportunities, and will not be successful. She suggests that trending analysis can be used as one of many tools in screening the merits of an NPD idea or marketing program.

In Vision Driving we go a step further. Trending analysis becomes one of the several stimuli in helping to generate new product ideas.

In our previous deconstruction of various innovations, we have seen where one factor driving many of these inspirations came from an awareness and understanding of the trends of the time. The more recent the innovation the more likely that trending analysis and application was one of the many factors in the ideation process.

SEARCHING OUTSIDE THE WHITE BOX FOR NEW PRODUCT INNOVATION

Vision Driving uses trend analysis as one of several stimulants in the NPD ideation process. In the last chapter we talked about the **Observation Tools.** Now we focus on the **Application Tools** by demonstrating how trends can create general opportunities. Later in this book I will show how these general opportunities can become the basis for creating specific NPD ideas for our business arena.

After observing any trend, we need to ask some questions. Who or what benefits from the trend, and who or what loses? Any trend will create both groups. By asking questions we place ourselves in the position of seeing ahead of the curve to determine the general threats and general opportunities, hopefully before it impacts our business. These questions and their answers are what I refer to as the ***Application Tools.***

In our example of more public display TVs we could see opportunities for cable companies to provide more targeted local advertising, community events notices, local traffic, and even precise local weather. As to the threats, this trend could be a threat to a national cable news networks if they are not the station selected to be on air in that public space.

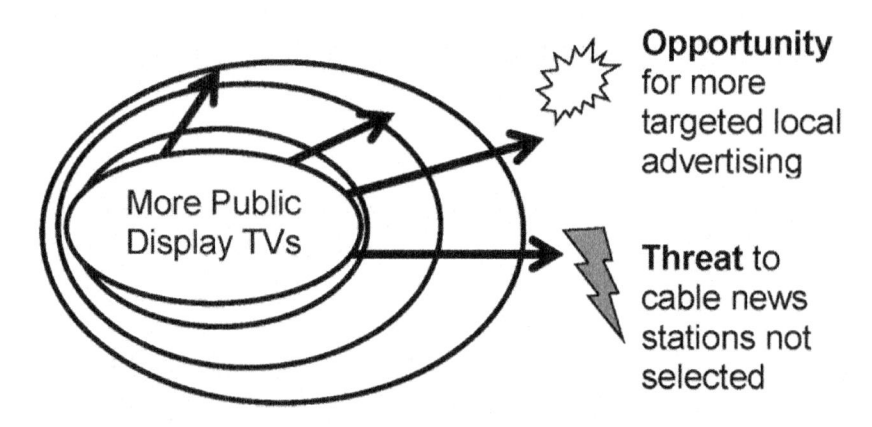

Opportunity for more targeted local advertising

More Public Display TVs

Threat to cable news stations not selected

The trend towards more natural ingredients creates opportunities for "healthier" products but threatens products with the "wrong" ingredients.

TRENDING ANALYSIS - APPLICATION TOOLS

Opportunity for healthier products

More Natural Ingredients

Threat to products with the "wrong" ingredients

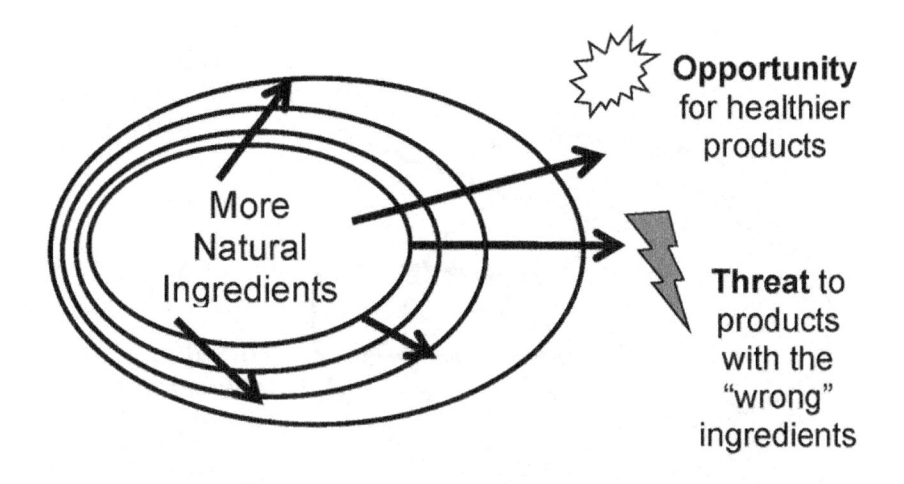

Reduced ozone layer threatens skin health, but creates demand for sun protection.

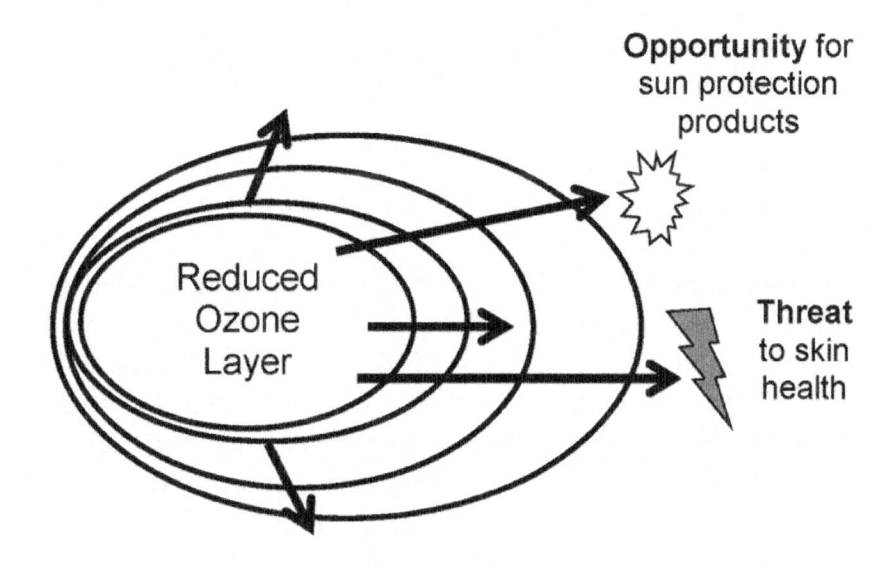

Opportunity for sun protection products

Reduced Ozone Layer

Threat to skin health

The rise in on-line purchasing is already having a huge effect on retailing.

◀ SEARCHING OUTSIDE THE WHITE BOX FOR NEW PRODUCT INNOVATION

Opportunity for all on-line merchants

Rising on-line purchasing

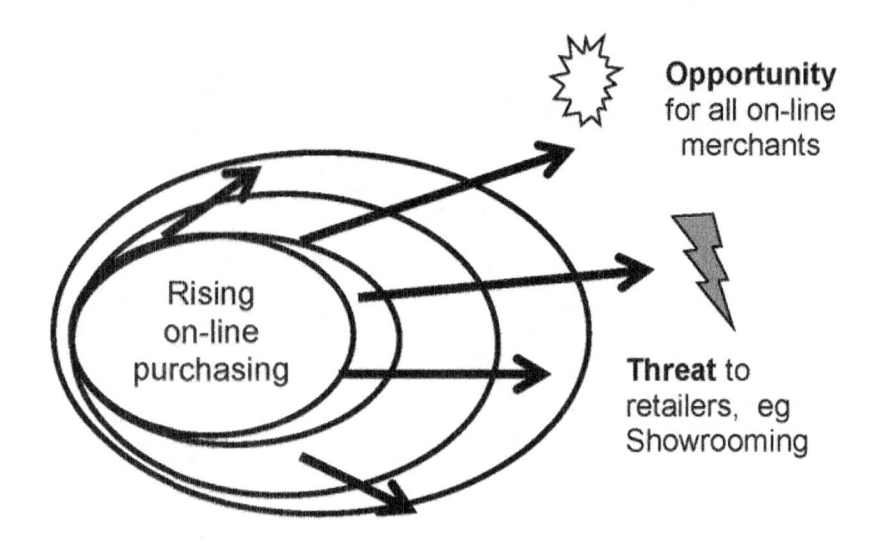

Threat to retailers, eg Showrooming

Extending health care to more people will create longer lead times to see a physician, but will increase demand for more accessible and cheaper alternative medical services (eg OTC Drugs, walk-in urgent care facilities, in-home diagnostics, etc)

Increasing crime threatens safety, but increases demand for home / personal security and public surveillance cameras.

In the Vision Driving process, we first create the list of trends from our observations and then assign each trend to one of the 4 groups mentioned earlier. Next, we want to identify the general opportunities that emerge from each trend, similar to the examples previously shown. We just have to connect the dots to find them. Later, in the Vision Driving process we can reference the list for our selected business arena to determine if these general opportunities can drive specific opportunities for NPD ideas within our arena.

Let's revisit the clusters of trends that we collected in the last chapter and see how each trend can drive a general opportunity.

TRENDING ANALYSIS - APPLICATION TOOLS

Marketplace: Media / Competition / Retailing

TRENDS	GENERAL OPPORTUNITIES
Growing appeal and use of on-line retailing; Retailers losing relevance; Showrooming	New ways for retailers to engage the consumer More in-store theatre Exploit benefits of face to face with consumer that is not available on-line All businesses can create new venues for on-line commerce
Need for more accessible and low cost medical services; Drug Chains offering more walk in medical services	Provide more on the spot medical testing and remedies for inside the Drug Chains Other retailers can find ways to offer more in-store services to offset losses to on-line shoppers
Growth of non-charge card payments such as Apple Pay ®	Greater range for commerce by small entrepreneurs etc
More organic products availability, & competition for Whole Foods ®	Organic anything may offer new opportunities
Growth of robot service assistants in retail (Lowes ®)	Robotic interactive devices and kiosks that offer in-store services and information Robotic use can extend into public spaces to provide information and assistance: eg police, fire, medical.

Marketplace: Media / Competition / Retailing

TRENDS	GENERAL OPPORTUNITIES
More media types in more places, both public and personal, and more interaction between them	Opportunity for more targeted advertising and information to the location
More advertising dollars moving from traditional media to "new media" such as social media, mobile, web, etc.	Opportunity for more targeted advertising to the consumer
More personalized / customized products & services	Any product or service has the opportunity to increase appeal and point of difference via customization
More immediate availability of items purchased on line (eg Amazon® same day delivery, FreshDirect ® food delivery)	Any business can add value with more immediate delivery of product or service
Mobil apps and connectivity between smart phones and retail transactions	Retailers can gain awareness and sales by connecting with consumer searches in real time
Growing 24/7 working class & lifestyles	More products and services available 24/7. Greater opportunity for public space vending kiosks or machines

TRENDING ANALYSIS - APPLICATION TOOLS

Consumer: Behavioral / Demographic / Societal

TRENDS	GENERAL OPPORTUNITIES
Changing " face " of retirement; more part time retirement, more retired population, more retirees free time	Products and services for older working people
Half of all meals are now eaten alone (but many with TV, IPad ®, Smartphone, newspaper, etc)	Interactive eating "companions" Interactive eating "entertainment"
More single households	Smaller size, single serve products
Increased clanning and sharing via texting, skyping, Facebook® and photo sharing such as Snapfish®, Shutterfly®, etc	New products or services to expand types of sharing
Increased use of specialized / customized virtual communities: singles like match.com ® , home owners like Angie's list ®, political candidates, political and health causes, etc	Every activity can have its own specialized group for support, information, advice, etc

Consumer: Behavioral / Demographic / Societal

TRENDS	GENERAL OPPORTUNITIES
Increased concerns for spread of diseases and food contaminations	Methods for consumers to prevent spread of germs Easy access for consumers to sterilize their food Methods to detect and keep homes germ free
As cost of living increases, consumers show continued interest in small low cost indulgences	Small pleasures like candies, nail salons, and other products or services that bring a moment of joy for low investment
Growing interest in electric cars	Public charging stations as locations for new venue for retailers Opportunity for ad media space
Less time spent in home cooking, while food consumption away from home is increasing	On the go food storage

TRENDING ANALYSIS - APPLICATION TOOLS

Consumer: Behavioral / Demographic / Societal

TRENDS	GENERAL OPPORTUNITIES
Use of shared transportation, ie car sharing and bike sharing: Car2Go®, Zipcar®, Citibike®, etc	Opportunities for more sharing in transportation, possibly in other forms such as the Segway®, in special locations What else can be shared?
Use of public surveillance cameras of people behavior	Opportunity for marketers and retailers to learn more about buyer behavior Possible use in trend spotting
Interest in healthy nutrition, organic foods	Anything organic and healthy may have appeal
Cashless transactions; Consumers carrying less cash (Apple Pay®,)	Easier for entrepreneurs to start up
Growth of Hispanics	More Spanish language use in packaging and retailing and advertising
Growing 24/7 working class & lifestyles	More 24/7 available products and services

Macro-Economic:
Industrial / Regulatory / Environmental

TRENDS	GENERAL OPPORTUNITIES
Rising health care costs	More cost effective alternatives to doctor visits
Inner cities reaching limits on congestion	Anything that reduces the number of cars used within a city
More disruptive weather	Personalized power supplies Longer lasting food storage
Continued reduction in the ozone layer	Opportunities for sun protection
More government intervention & controls	Services that help decipher rules and regulations
Increased threats from cyber hacking of companies, retailers, etc	More opportunities for security systems and services
Greater controls on greenhouse gases	Opportunities for products and services that reduce greenhouse gases

Macro-Economic:
Industrial / Regulatory / Environmental

TRENDS	GENERAL OPPORTUNITIES
Use of RFID wireless tracking devices	Applications to all things, living and not, that could add value or safety with location knowledge
Rising taxes	Personalized accounting services
Growth of solar panel use	Opportunities for more widespread use, lower cost, user friendly and adaptable
More use of public surveillance cameras	Opportunity for retailers to learn more about buyer behavior Possible use in trend spotting
More hostile world coming closer to home	Need for more instantaneous news. Personal safety, firearms, home security, emergency services etc Items for "off the grid" survival

Technology Trending: Inside & outside our arena

TRENDS	GENERAL OPPORTUNITIES
Growing use of portable devices	Customized marketing, more media ad options
Video Training	Brands hosting services
Growing use of public / environmental data gathering by multi-sensor surveillance (eg people movements, sound, temperatures, air quality, etc)	Opportunity for municipalities to apply resources economically Faster response time by first responders Retailers can access this info to better identify people traffic patterns for sales promotions
Growing use of Skype ™ and Google Plus®	More remote communications, solo and group
Emerging technology for social robots	Dedicated social robots for specific needs such as daily companions, family one-on-one Skyping, medical interactive robots, researcher aids, eating companions, etc
Growing use of Smartphones for medical condition sensors and self diagnosis, plus virtual contact with Physicians	Opportunities for new Smartphone apps Self diagnosis devices which attach to Smartphones

TRENDING ANALYSIS - APPLICATION TOOLS

Technology Trending: Inside & outside our arena

TRENDS	GENERAL OPPORTUNITIES
Growth of renewable energy sources and consumption: like wind, solar, wave, hydroelectric	Opportunities for more widespread use by making the systems less expensive, more user friendly, and adaptable
Increased applications for 3-D printing	Can make customized low cost one-off products
Connectivity: people to people, people to things, things to things	Anything can have more value with connectivity
Incorporating "smart technology" into traditional appliances, into home management, transportation, etc.	Anything can have more value with smart technology. Opportunities for more customized, personalized information and services
Wearable technology (eg Google® Glass, and Smartwatches)	More on the go intelligence. Bring more smart technology to anything we wear or take with us
Portable power sources Longer battery life	Take more stuff with you on the go to do more stuff

◄ SEARCHING OUTSIDE THE WHITE BOX FOR NEW PRODUCT INNOVATION

Technology Trending: Inside & outside our arena

TRENDS	GENERAL OPPORTUNITIES
Medical implants and miniature digestible internal sensors and Imaging	Monitoring, treating, diagnosing human conditions from within the body, without invasive procedures
Growing use of drones for business in delivery and aerial observations	Faster real time delivery for selected products Aerial viewing, for real estate, photography and surveillance
Growing use of Cloud storage	Opportunities for more accessible and usable data
Growth of Big Data	Better knowledge of behaviors and associations for application to all entities, government, business, schools, etc
GPS applications	Add GPS to anything where location or mobile location is of value Opportunities for tracking kids, animals, mentally disabled
Nanotechnology	Apply where small is a factor

Trending analysis is a dynamic activity. By the time this book is printed, the above list of trends and general opportunities will be much expanded. For this reason, this task should be conducted routinely and revisited continually for updates.

Trending analysis can be a powerful stimulus in the Vision Driving process. In the deconstruction of historical innovations we have seen that trends may have been one of the factors driving these innovations. As lines of communication have improved, we see that this factor has become more important. In the Vision Driving process

TRENDING ANALYSIS - APPLICATION TOOLS

we consciously and deliberately force our thinking to imagine how trends and the general opportunities they are creating can be distilled and directed towards creating specific NPD ideas in the arena under review. Pressure testing the list of general opportunities and asking how they can drive specific opportunities within the chosen business definition, can be a very productive Vision Driving tool.

CHAPTER 11

Challenging Beliefs

Great things happen when we challenge what is in front of us. Early Man took a long time to challenge the belief that the sun rises each day and rotates around the earth, or that the earth itself was flat. Once these beliefs were challenged and then substituted with more accurate ideas, the world changed. Man was humbled when he learned that the universe isn't centered on Earth, and Mankind was forever changed upon the discovery of the New World.

The difficulty in this task is that we live every day by a set of beliefs and often don't know it and more often don't question it. A heavier rock will fall faster to the earth than a lighter rock, we cannot see inside our bodies without surgery, salt water cannot be made drinkable, man cannot make something cold that isn't cold, body parts cannot be grown in a lab, gravity isn't reversible, teleportation is impossible, the blind cannot be made to see, the weather cannot be controlled, man cannot fly faster than the speed of sound, and so on. We believe these things, or we had previously believed these things before they were ultimately disproved, because it was conventional wisdom at the time. We tend not to question something that is implicitly accepted. The irony of these beliefs is that they are not always correct, or they are not always the only possible outcome.

CHALLENGING BELIEFS

Some of the greatest discoveries and inventions happened when someone challenged one of the beliefs at the time. People accepted the belief of spontaneous generation because it always worked, ie bugs and flies always appeared on dead animals left out in the open to rot. But, their belief was proven wrong by those who studied the phenomenon to learn that the bugs and flies were *attracted to the rotting meat*, and *not created by the rotting meat*. Columbus discovered America because he challenged the belief that the earth was flat. Einstein was the first to postulate the principle that light travels at a constant speed by first challenging the notion that time was a constant. As he explained it, time itself slows down when things speed up. (let that sink in for a moment for its monumental leap of intellect). When Google invented the glucose monitoring contact lens they had to challenge the belief that blood was the optimal marker for glucose levels.

The difficulty then is to recognize a belief, and the way to do this is to question everything. If we were intent on creating a new form of transportation, we would be confronted with the following beliefs:

- That transportation was a necessary thing in the first place (why do we travel?).

- That transportation requires vehicles.

- That transportation requires that we get into or onto something.

- That our bodies alone do not have the power to move faster than our feet.

- That transportation requires that our entire body moves to a new place.

◄ **SEARCHING OUTSIDE THE WHITE BOX FOR NEW PRODUCT INNOVATION**

Let's look at the last belief, ie that transportation requires that our entire body moves to the new place. This makes us think for a moment. What is transportation? Does our entire body have to be transported to be called transportation? I am not suggesting that we cut up our bodies and ship off the pieces one at a time. Instead, such questioning may drive us to a new meaning of transportation.

Question: If we can transport all or some of our faculties to a new location and have it communicate with ourselves in real time back to our original location, is this sufficient to be called transportation? If we can fully experience and interact with the new location by all our faculties without physically being there, is this transportation? Must the whole body travel for us to call it transportation? Or are we describing a more recent phenomenon, ie *virtual transportation?*

We already see examples of how this thinking has given birth to "bodiless transportation". We send mechanical probes to Mars to study the planet and send information back to us here on Earth. We have live Webinars that permit sight and sound to be shared in real time at a distance without our bodies moving to a new location. By transporting some of our faculties, we are able to achieve some of the benefits of full body transportation. In some cases that might be enough, and much more practical and economical. Hence the success of *GoToMeeting*.

Questioning beliefs is an exciting and productive step in the Vision Driving process. The above exercise took us beyond the questioning of beliefs about transportation. If we continued in the Vision Driving process to explore more nuances to the notion of transportation, we might end up creating the next disruption in transportation. We might for instance end up creating fully sensing robotic 3D avatars which are transported to a new location and are capable of "full faculty experiences " which are then transmitted in real time back to the original live individual in his/her initial

CHALLENGING BELIEFS

location. If we can fully feel that we are someplace else and doing something else, is that to be considered as transportation? Whether the answer is yes or no is not important. What is important is how by challenging beliefs we are able to stimulate our thinking about doing things differently, and in turn, helping us to create new disruptive transportation products.

Challenging beliefs is what got man to where he is now. In Vision driving it becomes one of many stimuli that can take us to the next big idea.

CHAPTER **12**

Borrowing and / or Combining Behavior

What is behavior? The American Heritage Dictionary cites a few definitions: "Actions or reactions of persons or things in response to external or internal stimuli; The manner in which something functions".

What makes this interesting is that by these definitions, behavior is a lot more than human behavior. Behavior is about functions, actions, reactions, or even no actions of just about anything as it exists in our universe, alive or not. A volcanic lava flow has a behavior. So does a raging river, a slow moving glacier, beavers building a log jam, the rotating earth in the void of space, a swarm of bees, smoke rising from a chimney, the engine in your car, Champaign fermenting in its bottle, an impenetrable wall when assaulted by a rocket (the no-effect behavior) , a flower turning towards the sunlight (heliotropism), or a rock falling to the ground. All of these describe a behavior that is either controlled from within the entity, or influenced from the external environment, or a combination of both.

Mankind's progress throughout history can in some way be linked to his insights gained from observations of such behavior. As examples, early man observed the behavior of the sun's rays and its motion throughout the day, the flow of a river in calm or stormy weather, and

BORROWING AND / OR COMBINING BEHAVIOR

migratory behavior of animals. He watched these things, and sought explanations for their behavior. With early man, the answer may typically have become the foundation for early myths, religion, and gods, like the sun gods. Later, as man began to study his world with more depth, he began to understand these behaviors with more accuracy than myth.

Today we stand on the shoulders of these people, as their observations and explanations of behavior became more accurate. Their observations of behavior, their learning that came from this, and their applications of these new insights, have helped mankind advance our standards of living from cave to modern cities. Today, this practice of observe-learn-apply has become far more sophisticated and specialized. Mankind has now divided this practice into many functional disciplines that pay attention to specific behaviors. A short list would include Sociologists, Psychologists, Engineers, Volcanologists, Meteorologists, Astronomers, Economists, Entomologists, and let's not forget Market Researchers who study consumer buying behavior.

As shown in previous chapters, the process of first observing, and then borrowing and/or combining behaviors, appears to be a common practice in the creation of inventions and innovations. In the Vision Driving process our intent is to proactively look for behaviors that we can borrow, and in some way combine or reconfigure into the creation of some new NPD ideas. There is truly a history of doing this all around us:

- The creation of radar and sonar was borrowed from the echo-location ability of bats.

- Was the Roman arch conceived by someone noticing the arch in our feet?

SEARCHING OUTSIDE THE WHITE BOX FOR NEW PRODUCT INNOVATION

- Archimedes screw was a simple device containing an elongated auger (a type of screw design) placed inside a cylinder, initially used beginning in the 3rd century BC for lifting water from a well. Today we see this concept borrowed and applied to the conveyance of grains, coals, and other granular material within industry.

- The electric light bulb as invented by Edison borrowed the behavior of a filament of conductive material as it would glow when an electric current is applied to it.

- Today's hydroelectric power plants have borrowed the idea that the energy of falling water can be harnessed, just as earlier man harnessed the same energy by using watermills.

- Nature has provided a means to help both predators and prey with the use of camouflage. Tigers have evolved to blend in with their jungle surroundings, while chameleons actually change color. Today, our military has borrowed this behavior and applied it to a range of scenarios.

- The OTC Drug Diphenhydramine was first used as an antihistamine in the 1940's to treat a range of symptoms such as allergies, colds, itchiness, and motion sickness. One of the side effects was its sedative properties. Today, we have many OTC Drug sleep aids that borrowed this side effect and made it the primary product benefit.

There is no limit to where we can look to observe behaviors of EVERYTHING to learn, borrow, or combine a behavior in the formation of new product ideas. This is a powerful tool to Vision Driving, and is limited only by the observation skills of the ideator or team.

BORROWING AND / OR COMBINING BEHAVIOR

So, how do we start? And where do we look for behaviors to borrow from? It all depends on the arena in review. And, there are several ways to approach this.

The most logical place to start looking for behaviors which might have bearing on the Vision Driving ideation process would come from the business definition and defined business arena. First, start by reviewing the key words in the business definition and mentally break it down into its dynamic parts.

- Let's use skin care for an example. If our business definition is "Protecting skin from the harmful rays of the sun", then consider what protection really means. Let's go with a simple definition of "something that prevents a harmful event from causing damage and/or pain". Can we borrow from other types or means of protection and apply it to our business of skin sun protection? Are there examples of protection in nature that we can borrow from? Are there examples of protection methods in specific groups of people in high risk situations where we can borrow and apply?

- In this same example, we could look at any phenomenon related to the sun for possible borrowing and application to skin sun protection. What would it mean to borrow from photosynthesis, heliotropism, the refraction of light rays as they pass through different media, the spectrum of light, the heat producing properties of sunlight, etc.?

- If our business arena is mobility we can look at all of nature where various challenges in mobility within different environments and terrains have already been met.

- If our business is in digestive aids, we can look at the behavior of fluids, the chemistry of adhesion, the dynamics of pipe design, and of course the world of biologics.

- If we are in the business of improving sight and vision, we should look at all types of optics, both living and man-made, as well as all phenomena and apparatus that allow us to see beyond the natural ability of our eyes.

While the above approach is a start, the next step in searching for behavior to borrow, is much more challenging. There is a world of behavior to borrow from if we can open our minds. Look everywhere, in other business arenas, different cultures, scientific principles, nature, etc. Look at other disciplines that study behavior as I listed earlier. If we were to look at our business arena as a Sociologist, or Engineer, or Astronomer, or Economist and others, then what behaviors would we identify as potentially applicable to our business?

Borrowing behavior is the more difficult and challenging tool than the borrowing of technology as discussed in the next chapter. But, this Vision Driving tool can be one of the most inspiring stimulants, and with the potential to drive some of the most disruptive NPD ideas.

CHAPTER **13**

Borrowing and / or Combining Technology

In Shakespeare's Hamlet we hear some good advice: *"Neither a borrower nor a lender be."* But in new product innovations, borrowing and or combining technology is a good thing. (By the way, lending can also be good, such as licensing out).

The idea of borrowing or combining technologies is age old, whether the action was sometimes conscious or not. History has many examples of this technique. The wheel and axle may have been invented by first observing the rolling properties of tree trunks, followed by several mental steps of borrowing and combining. Start by slicing off two discs from the ends of a large tree trunk (taking with them the borrowed rolling properties) and then joining (combining) these at their centers with a length of a narrower tree trunk (borrowing its rolling properties), and we have the first wheel and axle. I was not sure to include this as an example of borrowed behavior or technology, but it's here for now, as a borrowed technology.

One of the most famous examples of borrowing and combining technology is the invention of the first telescope. Various lenses, which at the time were used as magnifying glasses or eye glasses, were

SEARCHING OUTSIDE THE WHITE BOX FOR NEW PRODUCT INNOVATION

borrowed and combined into a series of lenses that made distant images appear large. This single invention was quite disruptive in that it led to the debunking of the belief that all things in the universe revolved around the earth. Sadly, Galileo paid a dear price for this theory as he was persecuted by the Church for blasphemy.

Another early example is the combination of gun powder, a metal tube, and a pellet, to create the first gun in the 1300's. This was clearly a disruptive idea that changed mankind forever. We see other historical examples:

- Combine a steam engine with a carriage and we see the first locomotive train.

- Many of Edison's inventions of sound devices borrowed the phenomenon that sound can cause electric impulses and visa versa.

- Modern photocopiers have their basis in the invention by Chester F. Carlson who was the first to have the vision that dry copying techniques would offer tremendous value to businesses. In 1937 he began work on his invention of the first photocopying machine. It took him over 10 years to find a company that would see its value of this new disruptive idea. Clearly his idea was not driven by any need-gap research of the time, which if it had identified such a need, would have accelerated the acceptance of his idea by potential manufacturers. Carlson's innovation embodied the notion of borrowing and combining various technologies and scientific principles to achieve his goal. Some of these included chemistry, electromagnetism, the process of photoconductivity, the behavior of light and its effect on certain chemicals, and an understanding of the fusing ability of heat, all combined to create the first dry photocopier.

BORROWING AND / OR COMBINING TECHNOLOGY

- Combine motion sensors with doors and we get automatic door openers, or combine it with sink faucets and we get automatic water dispensers.

- Borrow car shock absorbers and combine them with running shoes and we get spring loaded running shoes.

- The modern vacuum cleaner had its start with the combination of three technologies or principles: a) electric motors that can power fans, b) the sucking power of a vacuum, and c) the ability of various paper filters to allow air to pass through while allowing for the dust or debris to remain on the other side. House cleaning was never the same.

- And right in front of us right now we are all witnessing one of the most disruptive new innovations, which among other things has used the power of combining technologies, to create a new-to-the-world segment called the Smart phone. The emergence of the iPhone® by Apple® , a vision of its creator, Steve Jobs, has combined a range of technologies including GPS navigation, computer operating systems, wireless communication technology, advanced lithium-ion batteries, web browsing, digital video downloading, and others, plus advanced design features, to create the new world of Smart phones. Apple seems to be leading the way by having the vision and the ability to alter current paradigms by building upon existing technologies, and adding their own new advances, to configure new-to-the-world ways of doing things.

In the Vision Driving process we want to force this technique of borrowing and / or combining technologies to help us create disruptive new product ideas. As we will see, the range of technologies that we could potentially study for possible application to our business arenas

SEARCHING OUTSIDE THE WHITE BOX FOR NEW PRODUCT INNOVATION

is truly limitless. Many may not be appropriate nor applicable, but we won't know that until we study it and imagine the combinations. And, the mental process of making these potential combinations can be fun, exciting, and empowering, as it should be.

Today we see an enormous growth in the combination and application of new smart technologies with existing products and technologies to create a world of new products, many of them causing disruption within their segments.

Some of my ideas shown here are just a tease for stimulating your own imagination:

- If we combine GPS technology, with wireless access to weather conditions, along with portable batteries, plus an LED light, all embedded in the handle of a rain umbrella, could we create a rain forecasting umbrella whose handle glows when it sees rain in the forecast?

- Or staying with umbrellas, (this time a sun umbrella) can we combine solar cells, heliotropism sensors, portable batteries, and miniature motors to create sun umbrellas for the beach, backyard, or pool, that change angle and direction to follow the sun's trajectory throughout the day to maximize your shade from the sun, *without the need for you to get up from your chair?*

- Add the new technology of piezoelectricity (the ability of two thin plates that are repeatedly compressed and released to create an electric current) to the sole of shoes and we can create a renewable energy source for powering our mobile devices, *just by walking.*

BORROWING AND / OR COMBINING TECHNOLOGY

- Add smart technology and miniature batteries to pill containers to create pill reminder beeping containers. Or, add a different sound to remind us when it's time to renew a prescription. Or, what the heck, add wireless technology to the pill container so it can send a remote message to the pharmacy when it's time to renew the prescription, and then sound a beep alarm to remind us when the script is ready for us to pick it up at the pharmacy.

CHAPTER **14**

Mind Tools That Stimulate Imagination

In the Vision Driving process, it is the Mind Tools that build on the previous steps with a series of questions intended to stimulate the imagination beyond the obvious. The idea of Mind Tools has been discussed and described in a range of books on creativity, and has often been used in the world of industrial design, engineering, marketing, and other disciplines. Our intent is to apply these tools to our developing NPD ideas to help "complete the story" of the idea. There is no limit to these tools. Any mental tool that stimulates creativity is welcomed in the process.

Some of the important Mind Tools include:

- **Make it bigger or colossal:** What happens when we take anything and make it much larger than its current size or shape? Does it become more or less useful? Does this imagination force new associations? Does it create new applications? Was the first helium filled airship or dirigible first imagined as a very large toy balloon?

- **Make it smaller or miniature:** This is one of the most often cited stimuli used in NPD ideation. We have already described where the idea of miniaturization played a role in the creation of roller skates and wheeled luggage.

- **Reverse the thinking, process, sequence, assembly, etc:** If we change the way something is used or assembled, does it reveal any new benefits? If we reverse our perspective does the new orientation change our thinking? In our earlier example, Google used this technique when they were building new ideas for self diagnostic contact lenses that perform glucose level testing in the eyes. When analyzing the dynamics of the eyes, Google applied reversed mind thinking by exploring not what the eyes see, but rather, what we see in the eyes. What they found was that glucose levels can be measured on the eyeball. Something they would never have considered without this reverse thinking tool.

- **Change the usage scenario: Make it portable, useful in different day parts, climates, geographies, etc.** This is a traditional technique used by marketers to discover new uses and new users for their products. What would it mean to create binoculars for underwater usage? The first steam engines were fixed in place until someone found another use as in energizing transportation. With the first wristwatches, someone had to consider how to make clocks portable.

- **How does or would nature solve the problem?** There is no end to what we can learn and apply from nature. Chances are if nature has been presented with the problem, nature has found a solution, and one worth learning from. The Chameleon and some fish change color to their surroundings to hide from predators, hence camouflage. Nocturnal animals have developed acute night vision to help seek prey or avoid them, hence night vision glasses. Bats and some other animals use echolocation sounds and their return time delays to that help them locate prey, hence sonar and radar. Insects move over rough and uneven terrain, hence multi-legged extraterrestrial rovers.

SEARCHING OUTSIDE THE WHITE BOX FOR NEW PRODUCT INNOVATION

- **Add some benefits, parts or ingredients / Remove some benefits, parts, or ingredients.** There is nothing shocking here about adding benefits, but the idea of removing benefits is somewhat counterintuitive to what marketers typically seek. If properly applied, the idea of removing benefits can create a new product that may cost less, be easier to carry, and better able to focus on just one dedicated task.

- **How does a change of view alter our observations?** What does the product or problem look like from a worm's eye view, a bird's eye view, an inside view, etc. What can we apply from our view of the real world to our view within the virtual world.....and vice versa?

- **Make it adjustable or flexible.** What would it mean to take your product and make it softer, malleable, and compressible, etc? What if car bodies could be made to repel fender benders by adding a soft or compressive outer surface skin to the exterior? Would a back scratcher become more useful if a squeeze of the handle could either lengthen or shorten its reach on demand? We are already seeing the idea of flexibility at work in the world of smart wearables, where the use of flexible electronics and batteries can now be formed to accommodate the demands of active wear garments.

These are but a few of the Mind Tools that can be applied to the Vision Driving process. Although Mind Tools are shown as one of the last steps in the process, its usefulness and application can occur at any time during the 8 Vision Driving steps.

CHAPTER **15**

Vision Driving and Idea Mapping in a Company Setting

So how does all this work? How can the Vision Driving process be applied in the real world setting?

As with other mental problem solving processes, Vision Driving can be conducted by the solo ideator or by a team. It can be conducted in one sitting, or as I prefer, over a period of time, allowing for homework and incubation time. It can be conducted repeatedly for any given task, with each time generating different NPD ideas. If conducted within a team setting, the results will vary depending on the leader, the size of the team, the composition of the team, and the amount of time devoted to homework in-between steps.

Vision Driving can be put to paper using something akin to the Mind Mapping tool, originally invented by Tony Buzan in the 1960's as a way to visualize, build, and energize the mental process of creativity or problem solving. Mind Mapping uses a white paper of various sizes appropriate for the setting, from standard size for the individual, to large easel board size for conference room teamwork. The process places visual shapes and statements on the map, building from the starting point of the task through the mental connections created by the individual or team, on its way to solving a problem or creating an idea.

For Vision Driving, I use a tool I call Idea Mapping which becomes a visual representation of our NPD idea building process. It starts with the first step, Business Definition, and guides the individual or team participants through each of the Vision Driving steps, concluding with Idea Formation. The developing map is best done on paper for the solo ideator, or on an easel pad or board within a group, or on a wall if you have one of those erasable painted walls.

Depicting this process here is not easy since it can start anywhere and go anywhere, and in the real world should include the many thoughts that emerge along the way. Although the process is shown here in a neat clean flow, in the real world this might become quite busy looking like an octopus or mosaic. Bring it on. The more robust the discussion and visualization of the process, at each step, the greater the likelihood that the Vision Driving process will drive high quality disruptive NPD ideas.

Idea Mapping will involve some or all of the 8 Vision Driving Steps:

1. Clearly Defined Business and Objective.

2. Immersion in the arena.

3. Trending Analysis, Observations, & Applications.

4. Challenging Beliefs / What if's.

5. Borrowing and /or Combining Behavior.

6. Borrowing and/or Combining Technology.

VISION DRIVING AND IDEA MAPPING IN A COMPANY SETTING

7. Mind Tools that Stimulate the Imagination.

8. Idea Formation.

As mentioned earlier, there are caveats to the process.

- Not all steps will be appropriate nor helpful in all ideation sessions, but you won't know it until you force it into the mental ideation process.

- NPD ideas can emerge from any single or multiple steps in the process, without going the full distance. Not all steps are always required to generate disruptive NPD ideas. Still, it is possible that good ideas developed in the early steps can be built up to even better ideas through the full 8 step process.

- Although the steps are shown as a progression, there is no reason not to loop back and forth, as ideas are built up.

- The Vision Driving process can be applied over and over again for the same arena, generating different results.

- The time spent on the entire process as well as on each step will vary depending upon the business arena, the setting (ie team size and time clock constraints) and the task at hand. The time spent for homework and / or incubation time in-between the steps cans also affect the pace, timing, and success of the entire Vision Driving Process. The more time for incubation, the better the results.

Simplified Overview of the Vision Driving Process

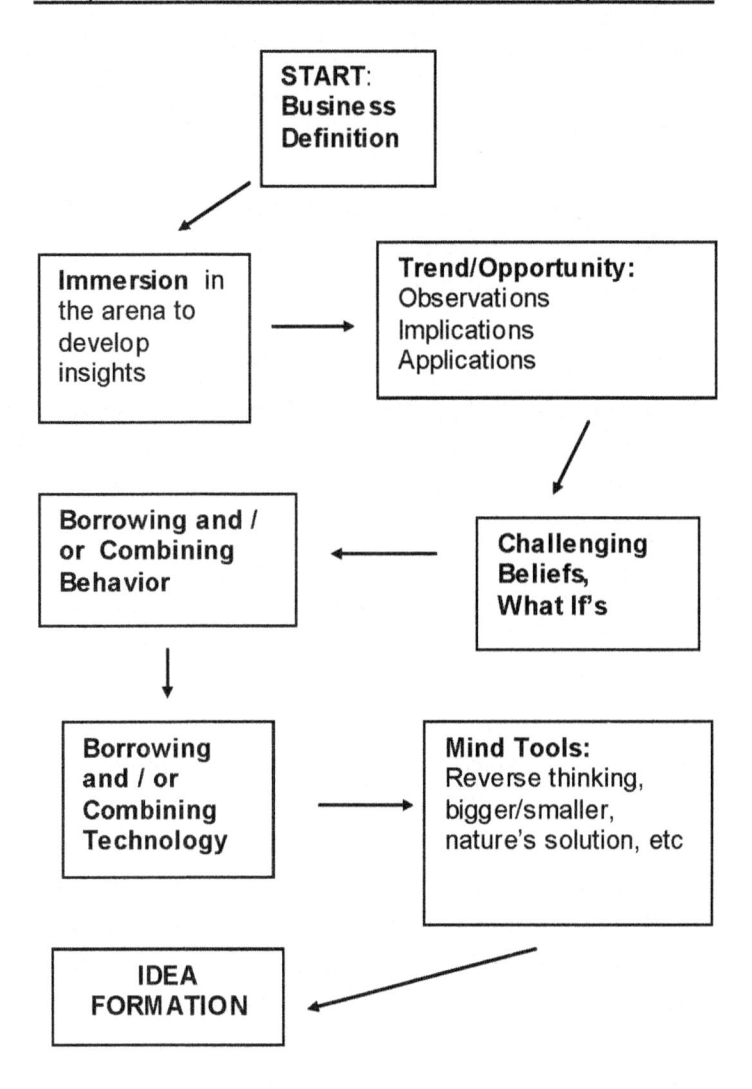

```
START:
Business Definition
   │
   ▼
Immersion in the arena to develop insights  ──▶  Trend/Opportunity:
                                                  Observations
                                                  Implications
                                                  Applications
                                                       │
                                                       ▼
Borrowing and/or Combining Behavior  ◀──  Challenging Beliefs, What If's
   │
   ▼
Borrowing and/or Combining Technology  ──▶  Mind Tools:
                                              Reverse thinking,
                                              bigger/smaller,
                                              nature's solution, etc
   │
   ▼
IDEA FORMATION  ◀──
```

As we go through this mapping process we must be reminded of what we are here for, ie to create new disruptive NPD ideas. Some of these ideas may include technology or technology applications that do not exist. That's OK. First, by creating the *idea* of the new technology we might be led to seek ways to invent it. Second, if the idea is strong

VISION DRIVING AND IDEA MAPPING IN A COMPANY SETTING

enough, we may want to find alternate ways of achieving the same or similar results with do-able technology today. This is a building process and every idea we generate can be viewed as a starting point for finding the better idea. If it can't be put into practice, then let's find a way to achieve the same or similar results with more creative thinking. If we want to stay ahead of our competition, we must embrace this mindset and approach.

How should Vision Driving be conducted to maximize the results?

For the solo ideator all that is required is a bunch of pads and pencils, and time spent in-between steps for homework and incubation time. This incubation period is vital, as it allows for new observations and connections that will enrich the Vision Driving exercise. The solo ideator has the advantage of carrying this process in her head wherever she goes and putting to paper whenever she wishes. It can take her whatever amount of time desired or can be conducted in a defined timeframe where there is a deadline. It can be done repeatedly, with each attempt building on the previous one, and generating different results.

When Vision Driving is conducted within a team setting, there are a number of factors to consider, each having an effect on the outcomes. Who should be in the team? Who should moderate? How should the steps be managed? And so on.

What follows is some guidance.

- The very first step is the selection of the business, or brand, or product arena, and the selection of the moderator, as agreed to by Senior Management.

- The chosen moderator or leader should be someone who is creative and imaginative, but properly grounded in the business realities. He or she should be a strong marketer with background in new product development. The person must be able to lead, provoke, stimulate, encourage, and inspire the team to become great thinkers, going well beyond the subject arena. She must be knowledgeable about the world in terms of trends inside and outside the arena, and comfortable with the technology of making products. The person should understand that her role is to provoke others to think, speak and contribute, rather than to dominate the sessions with her own thoughts.

- The room setting should include several easel pads up front and a set of tables for participants in the form of U shape with the open end facing front to allow the moderator to move into the U for closer conversations.

- The size of the team should be between 8 - 12 participants.

- Team participants should be individuals within or outside the company who exhibit an open and curious mind, and have the time to devote to the task.

- The composition of the team should be diverse: by age, by gender, by discipline. The mix is important. The group should not be limited to just marketing individuals or new product R&D staff. You want people from different functional areas and perspectives to make for the best interactions in building NPD ideas.

- All sessions should start with the Business Definition, followed by the Immersion step. But the sequence thereafter depends on the decisions of the moderator and the team. Steps can be repeated and looped back as the NPD ideas are developed.

VISION DRIVING AND IDEA MAPPING IN A COMPANY SETTING

- The actual time devoted to each step in the process is discretionary, but I prefer that each session focus on just one step and that the individual sessions should not be less than one hour each. People need time to acclimate to the team and the task at hand.

- It is likely that the team participants will generate new NPD ideas at any time and at any step in the Vision Driving process. This is expected and it should be allowed to happen. The moderator will have a choice of detailing the ideas on a separate "parking lot" easel pad, or by placing the ideas onto any of the developing Idea Mapping pathways. The benefit of the latter is that the new ideas can themselves become seeds for generating even more and possibly better ideas as further steps in Vision Driving stimulate new thinking.

- Just as with the solo individual, the time spent in-between the sessions for homework and incubation is part of the process and should not be discounted. I have found in my practice that incubation is a powerful factor in the success of the Vision Driving team exercise. The minimum time should be one week in-between sessions. Once a topic is chosen and the process begins, it is likely, and intended, that the team members will carry the process in their heads on a daily basis, whereupon new observations and new connections will emerge. We know that this works from historical examples of innovations. The more time spent in this incubation, the more likely that the Vision Driving process will produce more and better team generated ideas.

- The homework and incubation process in-between sessions is best conducted when assignments are divided among individual teams of 2 participants each.

SEARCHING OUTSIDE THE WHITE BOX FOR NEW PRODUCT INNOVATION

Here are some thoughts on how the moderator should conduct the Vision Driving process.

Pre-Session

- Team participants should be invited to the sessions and told the basic requirements and responsibilities for time spent and need for homework in-between sessions. The moderator should let the participants know in advance how many sessions will be conducted, over what period of time, and what is to be expected from them.

- After selecting the team participants and scheduling the first session, the moderator should advise the participants in advance of the chosen business arena in review and ask all participants to come to the first session with their idea of the business definition.

First Session

- Moderator to review objectives, ground rules, overview of the process, and the need for homework and incubation. Moderator to assign 2 person homework teams to ensure diversity.

- Moderator to write down all business definitions on front end easels, as prepared by participants before the first session.

- Discuss the 5 elements to a business definition, and formulate a business definition for the current business as it is today.

- Pressure test each element in the Business Definition, expanding each element to demonstrate the real world implications. Discuss options, pros and cons. Agree on a definition that allows for some expansion to the current business.

VISION DRIVING AND IDEA MAPPING IN A COMPANY SETTING

> **START:**
> **Business Definition**

- Moderator to review the need for Immersion in the business. Team to list the various perspectives on Immersion. Moderator to assign each perspective to a different 2 person team for homework.

Second Session

- Moderator to ensure that the Business Definition as agreed to in first session is clearly displayed at front of room.

- Participants to review homework assignments on Immersion.

- Moderator to write down key findings and Immersion insights on up front easels for each perspective and from each 2 person group.

- Moderator to start building the Idea Map with the Business Definition.

- Team to offer inputs on which Immersion insights may offer productive leads. Moderator to start building the Idea Map with the selected Immersion insights.

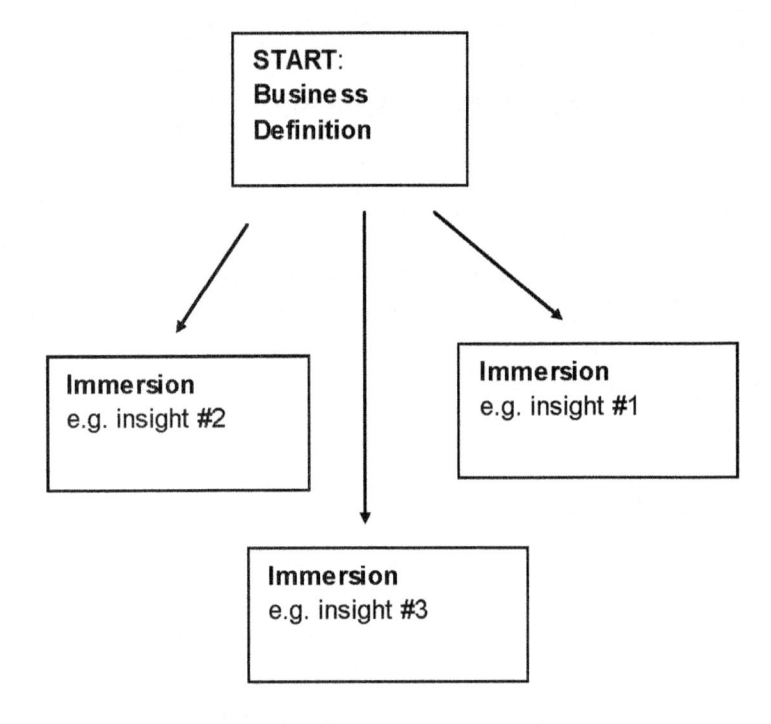

◄ SEARCHING OUTSIDE THE WHITE BOX FOR NEW PRODUCT INNOVATION

```
        ┌─────────────┐
        │ START:      │
        │ Business    │
        │ Definition  │
        └─────────────┘
         ╱      │      ╲
        ╱       │       ╲
┌──────────┐    │    ┌──────────┐
│Immersion │    │    │Immersion │
│e.g. insight #2│  │e.g. insight #1│
└──────────┘    │    └──────────┘
                ▼
         ┌──────────┐
         │Immersion │
         │e.g. insight #3│
         └──────────┘
```

- Moderator to provide overview on the importance of Trending Analysis in the Vision Driving process. Review the Observation Tools and the 4 types of trends, and demonstrate how trends create both threats and opportunities.

- Moderator assigns homework to 2 person teams to produce a list of observed trends within their assigned trend type.

Third Session

- Moderator to use easels to write down the lists of trends within the 4 types as provided by the 2 person teams.

- All team participants to contribute to further building the lists.

VISION DRIVING AND IDEA MAPPING IN A COMPANY SETTING

- Moderator to engage team to review lists and begin to generate General Opportunities for each trend from the list of observed trends within each of the 4 types.

    o **Marketplace:** Media / Competition / Retailing

    o **Consumer:** Behavioral / Demographic / Societal

    o **Macro-Economic:** Industrial / Regulatory / Environmental

    o **Technology Trending**: Inside & outside our arena

Trend Type: Example: **Marketplace**

TRENDS	GENERAL OPPORTUNITIES
Example	Example Example
Example	Example Example

- Team to assist Moderator in building Idea Map now using selected Trend/Opportunities from the lists.

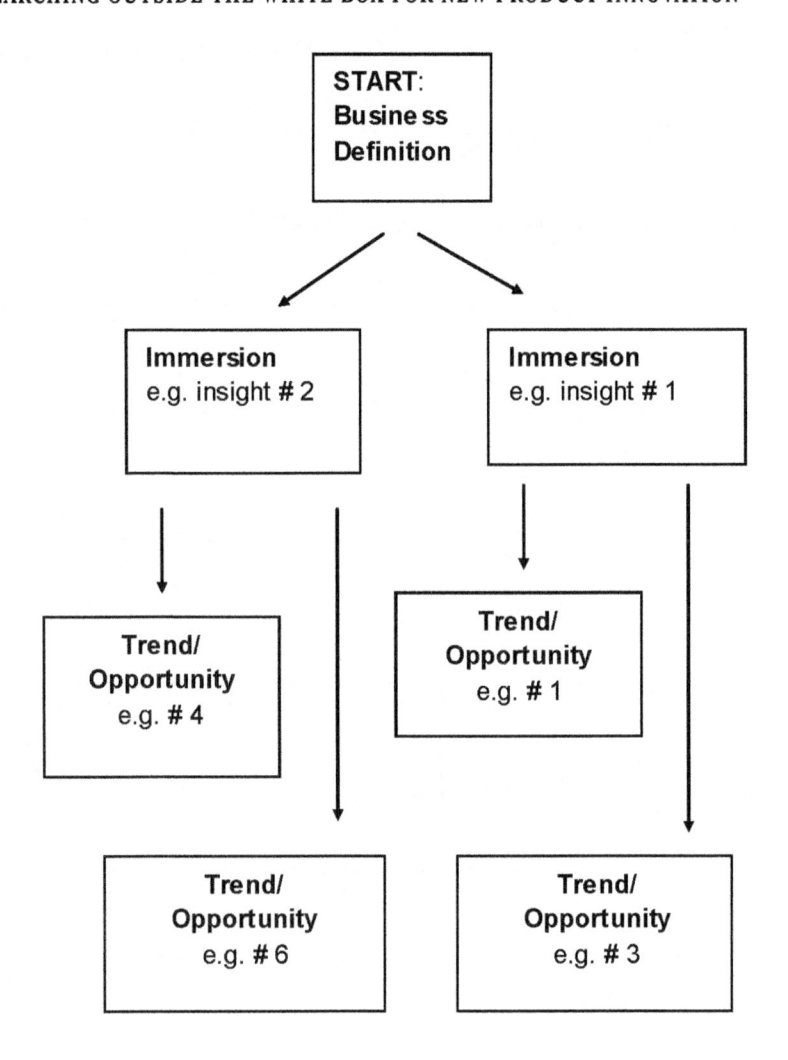

◂ SEARCHING OUTSIDE THE WHITE BOX FOR NEW PRODUCT INNOVATION

```
                    ┌─────────────┐
                    │   START:    │
                    │  Business   │
                    │ Definition  │
                    └─────────────┘
                      ↙       ↘
        ┌─────────────┐       ┌─────────────┐
        │  Immersion  │       │  Immersion  │
        │e.g. insight#2│      │e.g. insight#1│
        └─────────────┘       └─────────────┘
              │   │                 │
              ↓   │                 ↓
        ┌─────────────┐       ┌─────────────┐
        │   Trend/    │       │   Trend/    │
        │ Opportunity │       │ Opportunity │
        │  e.g. #4    │       │   e.g. #1   │
        └─────────────┘       └─────────────┘
                  │                     │
                  ↓                     ↓
        ┌─────────────┐       ┌─────────────┐
        │   Trend/    │       │   Trend/    │
        │ Opportunity │       │ Opportunity │
        │  e.g. #6    │       │   e.g. #3   │
        └─────────────┘       └─────────────┘
```

- Without coaching, the Moderator to allow team participants to spontaneously create NPD ideas if they so wish. As mentioned before, the moderator will have a choice of detailing the ideas on a separate "parking lot" easel pad, or by placing the ideas onto any of the developing Idea Mapping pathways. The benefit of the latter is that the new ideas can themselves become seeds for generating even

VISION DRIVING AND IDEA MAPPING IN A COMPANY SETTING

more and possibly better ideas as further steps in Vision Driving stimulate new thinking.

- Moderator to introduce the notion of Challenging Beliefs and its importance, and offer examples. Team is asked to come up with one or two beliefs that can be challenged in this arena. Homework is assigned to the 2 person teams to generate a further list of beliefs and What If's that have bearing on this business arena.

Fourth Session

- Moderator to ask each 2 person team to recite their list of Beliefs and What If's and write them down on upfront easels.

- Moderator to display the Idea Map from last session. Team is asked to look at each of the pathways and select any one of the Challenged Beliefs and What If's, that provoke thinking. Continue this exercise for other pathways, and / or other Challenged Beliefs/What If's.

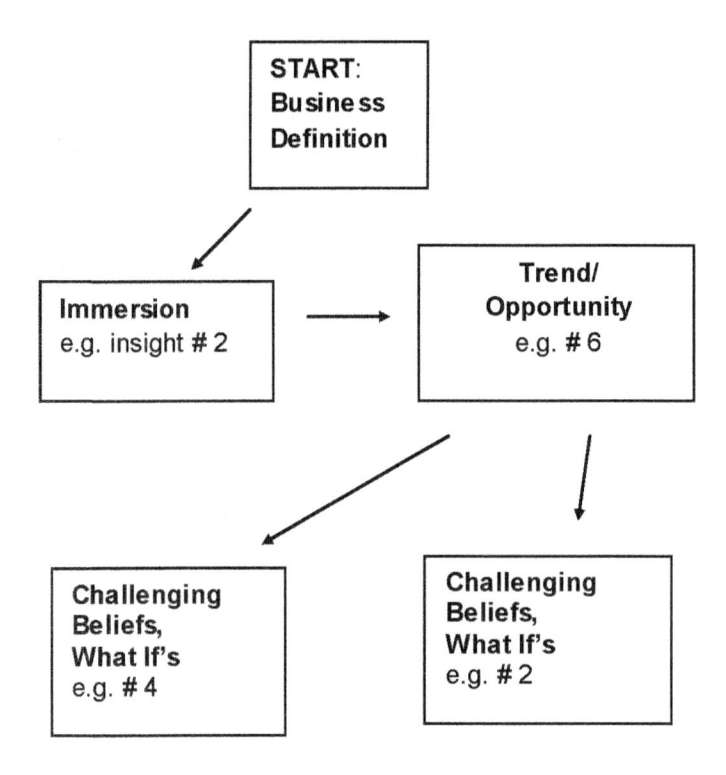

SEARCHING OUTSIDE THE WHITE BOX FOR NEW PRODUCT INNOVATION

```
                    ┌─────────────┐
                    │   START:    │
                    │  Business   │
                    │  Definition │
                    └─────────────┘
                      ↙         ↘
        ┌──────────────┐    ┌──────────────┐
        │  Immersion   │ →  │   Trend/     │
        │e.g. insight #2│   │ Opportunity  │
        │              │    │  e.g. #6     │
        └──────────────┘    └──────────────┘
                    ↘         ↓
        ┌──────────────┐    ┌──────────────┐
        │ Challenging  │    │ Challenging  │
        │   Beliefs,   │    │   Beliefs,   │
        │  What If's   │    │  What If's   │
        │   e.g. #4    │    │   e.g. #2    │
        └──────────────┘    └──────────────┘
```

- It may become helpful for the moderator to begin to isolate the developing Idea Mapping pathways onto separate wall sheets.

- Continue to develop pathways until connections are exhausted.

- Moderator to talk about the idea of Borrowing or Combining Behavior and offer examples. Team to offer examples as well. Homework is assigned to the 2 person teams to identify any/all behaviors that may have bearing.

VISION DRIVING AND IDEA MAPPING IN A COMPANY SETTING

Fifth Session

- Participants to identify their lists of Behaviors for consideration. Moderator to list them on the upfront easels.

- Entire team to pressure test all behaviors and ask what a Borrow or Combination to any of the developing Idea Mapping pathways would mean.

- Moderator to provoke team to make connections.

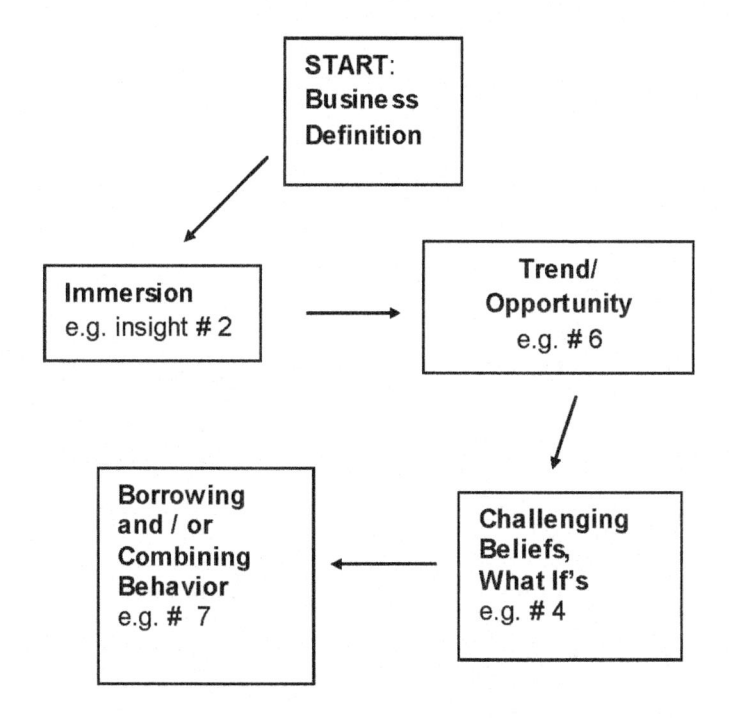

```
         ┌─────────────┐
         │ START:      │
         │ Business    │
         │ Definition  │
         └─────────────┘
         ↙              ↘
┌──────────────┐   ┌──────────────┐
│ Immersion    │ → │ Trend/       │
│ e.g. insight │   │ Opportunity  │
│ # 2          │   │ e.g. # 6     │
└──────────────┘   └──────────────┘
                          ↓
┌──────────────┐   ┌──────────────┐
│ Borrowing    │   │ Challenging  │
│ and / or     │ ← │ Beliefs,     │
│ Combining    │   │ What If's    │
│ Behavior     │   │ e.g. # 4     │
│ e.g. # 7     │   │              │
└──────────────┘   └──────────────┘
```

- Moderator to provide overview and examples of Borrowing or Combining Technology.

- Team to begin to offer ideas for technologies that might have merit in this business arena. Moderator to provoke team to think of very diverse technologies outside of this business arena.

◄ SEARCHING OUTSIDE THE WHITE BOX FOR NEW PRODUCT INNOVATION

- Moderator assigns homework for 2 person teams to generate lists of broad range of technologies to consider.

Sixth Session

- Participants to list their ideas for Borrowing or Combining Technologies and Moderator to list these on upfront easels.

- Moderator to bring team attention to each of the developing Idea Mapping pathways to provoke discussions about connecting various technology applications.

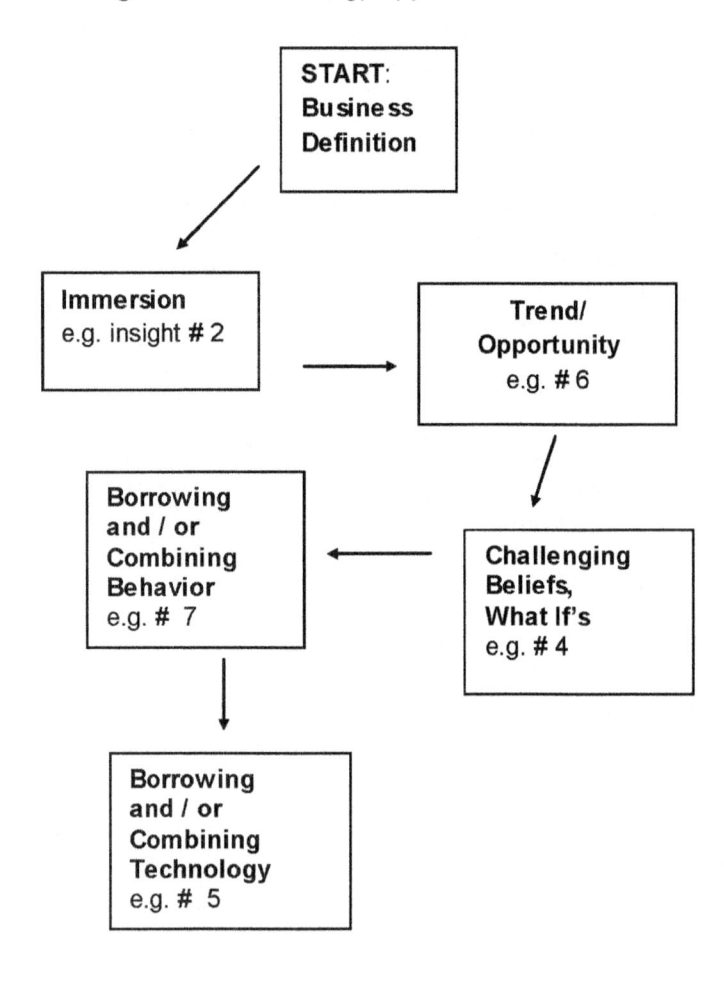

```
                    ┌──────────────┐
                    │ START:       │
                    │ Business     │
                    │ Definition   │
                    └──────┬───────┘
                           │
                           ▼
    ┌──────────────┐                ┌──────────────┐
    │ Immersion    │                │ Trend/       │
    │ e.g. insight │ ─────────────► │ Opportunity  │
    │ # 2          │                │ e.g. # 6     │
    └──────────────┘                └──────┬───────┘
                                           │
                                           ▼
    ┌──────────────┐                ┌──────────────┐
    │ Borrowing    │                │ Challenging  │
    │ and / or     │                │ Beliefs,     │
    │ Combining    │ ◄───────────── │ What If's    │
    │ Behavior     │                │ e.g. # 4     │
    │ e.g. # 7     │                └──────────────┘
    └──────┬───────┘
           │
           ▼
    ┌──────────────┐
    │ Borrowing    │
    │ and / or     │
    │ Combining    │
    │ Technology   │
    │ e.g. # 5     │
    └──────────────┘
```

VISION DRIVING AND IDEA MAPPING IN A COMPANY SETTING

- Moderator to describe the use of Mind Tools to stimulate thinking. Various examples are offered, and the team is encouraged to add their thoughts.

- Moderators to ask team participants to write down their favorite Idea Mapping pathways, along with what they think are the most intriguing Vision Drivers. The homework assignment is to use the Mind Tools and selected Vision Drivers to generate Idea Formation of new NPD ideas.

Seventh & Final Session

- Moderators to ask each 2 person team to go upfront in the room to the various Idea Mapping pathways and build their own Idea Formation descriptions using Mind Tools and other Vision Drivers as appropriate.

- If there are any Idea Formation NPD ideas developed along the way that were placed in the "Parking Lot" easel, these should be brought back into the appropriate Idea Mapping pathways.

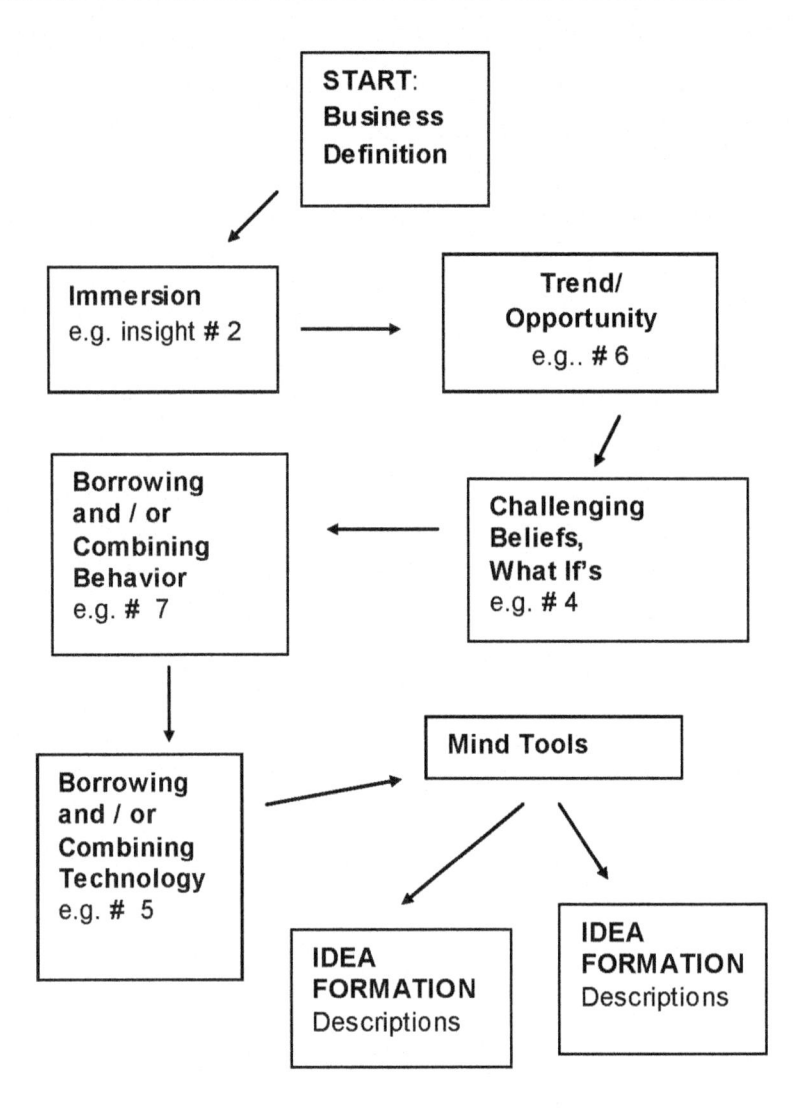

◄ SEARCHING OUTSIDE THE WHITE BOX FOR NEW PRODUCT INNOVATION

```
START:
Business Definition
    │
    ▼
Immersion               →    Trend/Opportunity
e.g. insight # 2              e.g.. # 6
                                   │
                                   ▼
Borrowing and / or      ←    Challenging Beliefs,
Combining Behavior           What If's
e.g. # 7                     e.g. # 4
    │
    ▼
Borrowing and / or      →    Mind Tools
Combining Technology         ╱        ╲
e.g. # 5                    ▼          ▼
                      IDEA FORMATION   IDEA FORMATION
                      Descriptions     Descriptions
```

- All participants to then review each pathway, one by one, to build on the presented NPD ideas.

- The team helps the Moderator to list each new NPD idea on a separate easel pad.

VISION DRIVING AND IDEA MAPPING IN A COMPANY SETTING

- Moderator concludes the program. Thanks the participants and encourages them to continue this process after today.

- Moderator provides Senior Management with a detailed report on the findings from the Vision Driving process.

The Vision Driving process as I have described it in this book has the potential to expand in terms of the range of stimuli that can be applied. From my experiences, once a team becomes completely immersed in the creative power of this process, the team might find itself creating other stimuli to build on the 8 steps shown here. When this happens, it is a sign of an empowered team, clearly capable of using the Vision Driving process to fulfill the NPD strategy that brought them here.

CHAPTER **16**

Vision Driving Applications

We now come to the point where we can exemplify the whole process of Vision Driving as a way to generate new disruptive NPD ideas in the Expansion Space. The Vision Driving process can be applied to almost any economic activity. In each of these examples I show how the process might look if we were in these business arenas and made certain assumptions about our business definitions and goals. I then offer my own set of talking points for each of the Vision Driving steps to suggest what might be generated by any solo ideator or company team. From these talking points I then build the Vision Driving Idea Map to show what could emerge in the Idea Mapping exercise to drive some new disruptive NPD ideas.

The NPD ideas in these examples will cover a range of possible NPD disruption. Some of the ideas will reflect modest disruption, while others are new-to-the-world product ideas which would have greater impact. Some suggest technology or technology applications that may be viable today, while others reflect technology that has yet to be created. I have selected only a very few examples of what can be done in each arena to offer a sense for how the process might work.

VISION DRIVING APPLICATIONS

As you review these examples, remember the objectives of Vision Driving:

1. It is designed to stretch our imagination in generating disruptive NPD ideas.

2. It is capable of stimulating a range of ideas to satisfy the need for a healthy volume of NPD ideas at the front end of the NPD stage-gate process.

3. The developed NPD ideas can create the descriptions of new technology and/or technology applications, *before the consumers ask for it.*

4. The NPD ideas with their new technology or technology applications can become the basis for motivating the actual creation of the new technology that may not yet exist.

5. The NPD ideas may offer the business incentive for identifying derivative ideas that use more viable, do-able today technology, while still maintaining sufficient appeal and revenue potential.

These examples reflect how the process might look as I conduct it as a solo ideator. When you look at my discussion points preceding the Idea Maps shown here, it will become apparent that my Idea Mapping examples reflect only a very few of the possible Vision Driver discussion points. What I show is only a small sample of what could be developed by a company team during their team discussions and from their own incubation and homework. And, that's a good thing. The discussions and talking points are only limited by the dedication and imagination of the team, and the skills of the moderator in provoking and inspiring the staff. And as a result, there are many more NPD ideas that can be generated for each arena.

◀ SEARCHING OUTSIDE THE WHITE BOX FOR NEW PRODUCT INNOVATION

But there is more to it.

This would be a perfect time for you to test your Vision Driving skills in building on what I have shown here, and make them your ideas. Start with the business arenas that I have selected and the talking points that I have shown. Next, build on them with your own talking points for each of the Vision Driving steps. Then, apply your new discussion points to the Vision Driving Idea Map to build your own NPD ideas for that arena. As you repeat the entire process you will continue to add your own talking points to each of the Vision Driving steps, and make completely new connections in driving new NPD ideas.

Finally, after going through the above exercise within those selected business arenas, task yourself and your company team to apply the Vision Driving method to your own businesses to generate NPD ideas. That is what this guide is for. You will find the process empowering and exciting in helping you and your company get out in front of the competitive change curve in identifying disruptive NPD ideas.

Have fun and good luck!

CHAPTER **17**

Vision Driving Applications - Foot Products

The very first step is to define our arena of interest, ie what business are we in and where do we want to search for new product ideas? For our purposes here we will first focus on consumer products. Let's start with a fictitious company that provides products for the feet.

Start by **Defining our Business** as products or services that protect feet, or improve foot health, and foot performance, targeted to all adults, and as products, they are sold through retail and on-line outlets and manufactured by contract manufacturers, and as services, delivered to consumers by whatever means. That's a pretty broad business definition.

Foot products and services can offer a range of benefits including those that promote healthy feet, faster feet, ways to keep feet clean, dry, and protected, high performing feet, good looking, nice smelling feet, and foot comfort and pleasure. Here is a segment that is broad enough in its scope to contain items that can each respectively satisfy just about any level within the Maslow's Hierarchy of needs. Seeing this robust range of needs associated with feet, we must now

◀ **SEARCHING OUTSIDE THE WHITE BOX FOR NEW PRODUCT INNOVATION**

determine where our business falls within this range, and where we want to focus for our growth.

- Is it our business to pursue products that help maintain the ability of our feet to keep us mobile so we can meet basic needs? That would be a pretty broadly defined business.

- Is it our business to protect feet, in all types of conditions, terrains, climate, time of day, time of year? This is also broad, but less so than the first.

- Are we here to reduce pain in the feet, or bring pleasure to the feet so they perform better?

- Are we in the foot appearance business?

- Are we in the foot performance business, with things that help our feet perform in our job as we earn a living and feed our family, or achieve the pride and esteem of being the best at something?

    o Do our products improve competitive performance for athletes?

    o Or... Do our products help improve performance for construction workers, police officers, military, lifeguards, cashiers, retail workers, etc?

For this exercise, we will make our decision to define our business more narrowly and more specific than our opening definition. We are in the business of providing foot products or services that improve comfort and performance for adults who work on their feet. If products, they are sold through retail and on-line outlets and manufactured by contract manufacturers, and if services, delivered to consumers by whatever means.

VISION DRIVING APPLICATIONS - FOOT PRODUCTS

These people might include: Factory workers, teachers, police, retail workers, waiters and waitresses, nurses, flight attendants, construction workers, museum guides, hair dressers, letter carriers, etc. It is indeed a long list, each group with slightly different needs, making this exercise a real challenge, and hopefully a lot of fun.

Immersion in the arena is intended to ground our thinking in all matters affecting feet. The goal is to broaden our view of feet, beyond the obvious, and beyond our own world view of feet. Such an approach will help us build on insights and stretch our ability in the Vision Driving process to create more innovative new product ideas.

For instance, we need to understand the way the foot functions, how the environment affects feet (indoor and outdoor), what demands are placed on feet in day to day life for a range of people and range of occupations, who the leaders are in foot care, what differences exist in feet from person to person, etc.

We need to look at the world of existing foot care products and services available and understand the competitive landscape, the various business models and product life cycles for any of the various sub-segments. We also need to learn about our target groups, their lifestyles, current behavior about their feet, and their respective special needs and products used.

For this exercise example we might want to know or guess how early man cared for his feet. What is the basis for Reflexology? What is the importance of the arch in humans? What are the typical foot problems? Do toes function in any ways like our fingers? How is the pressure on the foot different as we walk, run, or simply stand?

When we add all this together, we have a well-defined business definition and target, as well as a complete immersion in the topic, in this case feet. We become experts not just in human feet and current means of foot care, but in the larger context of *all things feet*. The broader our new perspective on feet, the more we are able to conceive ideas that go beyond current need-gaps, current practices, and even current technologies in foot care.

The **Trending Analysis** step and its implications for General Opportunities will be essentially the same for all Vision Driving experiences. The overview of some selected trends and their associated general opportunities have been covered in a previous chapter. By the definition, these general opportunities will present themselves to us for whatever our chosen Vision Driving arena. Our task in the Vision Driving process for any selected business arena is to then re-visit the list of trends and general opportunities and determine how these can drive specific NPD ideas for our business arena.

With some pressure testing and imagination we might see how some of these trends may offer immediate stimulation for NPD ideation in our foot care arena, for instance:

- The growing appeal of customization and personalization.
- Use of smart technology in anything.
- Use of long lasting portable batteries.
- Growing appeal of wearable technology.
- Use of 3-D Printing.
- Growth in available walk-in services.
- Continued appeal of small indulgences.

VISION DRIVING APPLICATIONS - FOOT PRODUCTS

If these or other trends can drive the creation of new product ideas, we will see this in the Idea Mapping exercise.

Challenging Beliefs is tough here, but if we are talking about helping provide comfort and performance to people who work on their feet, where is it written that the feet must carry the entire load bearing weight? That may sound odd but it raises the question of how the weight bearing burden of feet might be reduced if transferred in part to something else, to help relieve some of the cause of foot discomfort. Actually, some people are already doing this. People who walk with a cane or use crutches or braces are reducing the weight bearing burden on their feet. And more recent advances in exoskeletons which help non ambulatory people to walk, also come to mind here. Can this notion have application to our task?

Another belief is that shoes must be store bought from what is made available by manufacturers. And, once bought, shoes cannot be customized in shape, performance, or comfort for the demands or activity without adding some sort of insert. Why can't shoes be self customized as the need arises from conditions or activity? Another belief is that foot massages can only be done with shoes off, and in special places like spas, massage parlors, and nail salons. Why can't I have my feet massaged when and where I want it, while still wearing shoes?

When we think about **Borrowing and or Combining Behavior** we want to look at any behavior that can improve foot comfort or performance. There are already a host of foot related comfort behaviors, such as insertable gel insoles, massage machines or baths, massage parlors or nail salons that offer foot massage services, and special orthotic shoes custom made to improve foot comfort and performance. Can we borrow from any of these to create some new disruptive NPD ideas?

◄ SEARCHING OUTSIDE THE WHITE BOX FOR NEW PRODUCT INNOVATION

For **Borrowing and or Combining Technology** we can look at an entire world of technology and ask: how can this be used in foot comfort? The only limit to what we consider is our knowledge of the world of technology and our imagination. What technology exists for improving comfort in a specialized way to the user? What would it mean to borrow the idea of self adjustable bed mattresses with their ability to customize support to the users needs? Car seats have an adjustable lumbar support feature that allows drivers to adjust the support for customized comfort. There is a new world of 3-D Printing that offers a low cost means to build just about anything in one-offs or multiples. New technology for portable batteries continues to improve features in size, weight, shape and duration of battery life. Can any of these have merit in improving foot comfort?

Another fascinating emerging technology to contemplate is piezoelectricity. This is the name for electrical current energy that is produced between two opposing surfaces when a pressure is applied to compress them together, and then followed by a removal of that pressure. The process creates a slight electrical current between the surfaces. Applications are just now being sought for such things as sidewalks and even dance floors used to energize lighting. What if we can borrow this phenomenon and then miniaturize it for use in a shoe so that every walking step produces a small electrical current? Can this energy be used to power foot massages or foot warmth on demand? What other benefits could we create?

When we look at other technologies where ground contact performance is a factor, we have an enormous field of study. What can we borrow from nature? What can we learn from vehicles and their tires? One intriguing fact that I have uncovered is that deflating the tires on army vehicles that landed on the beaches of Europe in the Second World War made it easier to drive them on the sand. The pressure in the tires was changed as needed to accommodate the terrain. Can we borrow this dynamic for footwear to change the bottom tread traction profile as the terrain demands change?

One of the **Mind Tools** that might be useful here is to ask if there are currently technologies, products, or services that can be made smaller and brought into the home. Can we create footwear products that are produced in the home, on-demand, at low cost, and customized to the user's needs? What would an on-demand miniature shoe factory in the home mean to our consumer? Other Mind Tools might present themselves during our Vision Driving process.

Now comes the fun part where we begin to poke, build, stimulate, and force the creation of new product ideas. We start with the refined Business Definition from our above exercise and then proceed through the Vision Driving steps. It should be obvious that we already have a bunch of ideas that will be further developed in this process.

At this point we want to put our thinking down on paper as an Idea Mapping exercise. Remember:

- Idea Mapping as shown here is a short contraction of what the process might look like in the real world.

- Not all steps will be appropriate nor helpful in all ideation sessions.

- NPD ideas can emerge from any single or multiple steps in the process, without going the full distance.

- Although the steps are shown as a progression, there is no reason not to loop back and forth, as ideas are built up.

- The Vision Driving process can be applied over and over again for the same arena, generating different results.

IDEA MAPPING (Foot Products 1)
Foot comfort & performance for people who work on their feet

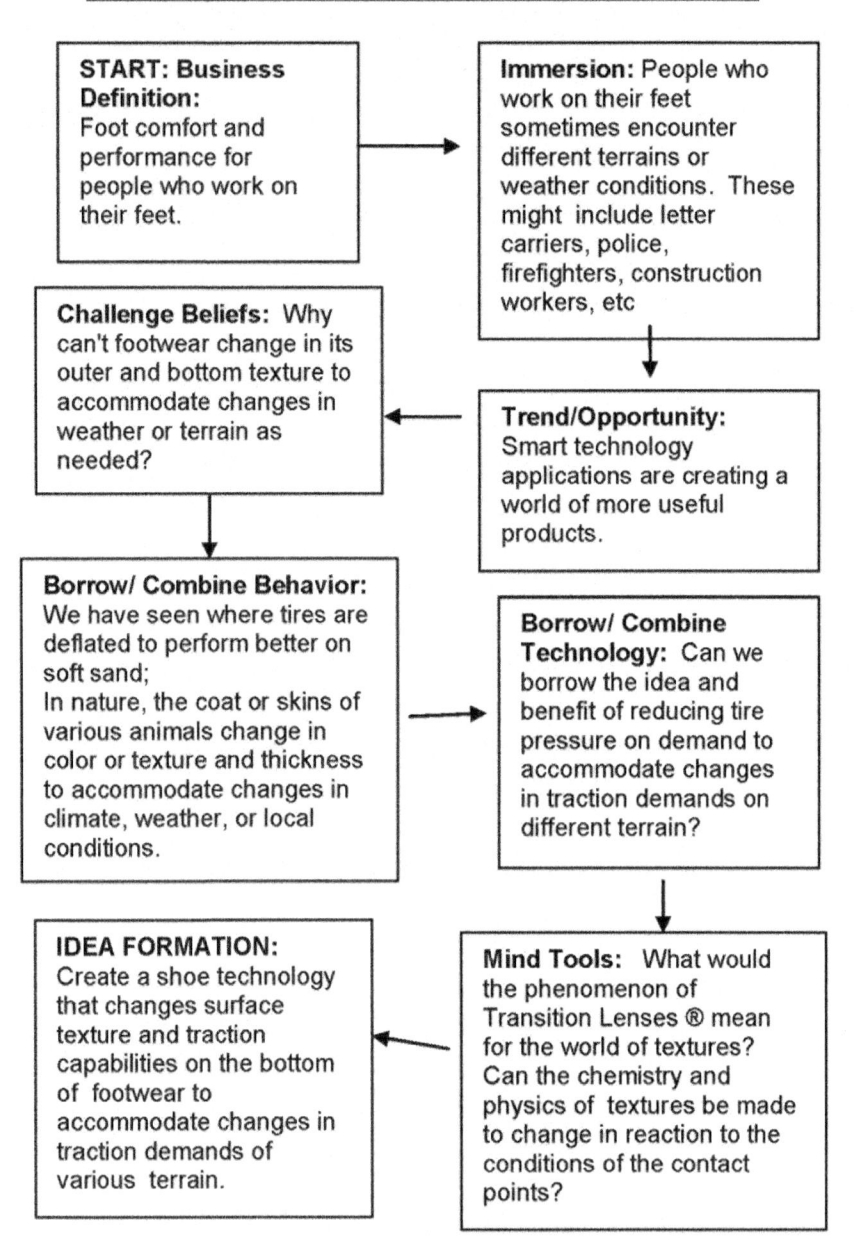

START: Business Definition: Foot comfort and performance for people who work on their feet.

Immersion: People who work on their feet sometimes encounter different terrains or weather conditions. These might include letter carriers, police, firefighters, construction workers, etc

Challenge Beliefs: Why can't footwear change in its outer and bottom texture to accommodate changes in weather or terrain as needed?

Trend/Opportunity: Smart technology applications are creating a world of more useful products.

Borrow/ Combine Behavior: We have seen where tires are deflated to perform better on soft sand; In nature, the coat or skins of various animals change in color or texture and thickness to accommodate changes in climate, weather, or local conditions.

Borrow/ Combine Technology: Can we borrow the idea and benefit of reducing tire pressure on demand to accommodate changes in traction demands on different terrain?

IDEA FORMATION: Create a shoe technology that changes surface texture and traction capabilities on the bottom of footwear to accommodate changes in traction demands of various terrain.

Mind Tools: What would the phenomenon of Transition Lenses ® mean for the world of textures? Can the chemistry and physics of textures be made to change in reaction to the conditions of the contact points?

VISION DRIVING APPLICATIONS - FOOT PRODUCTS

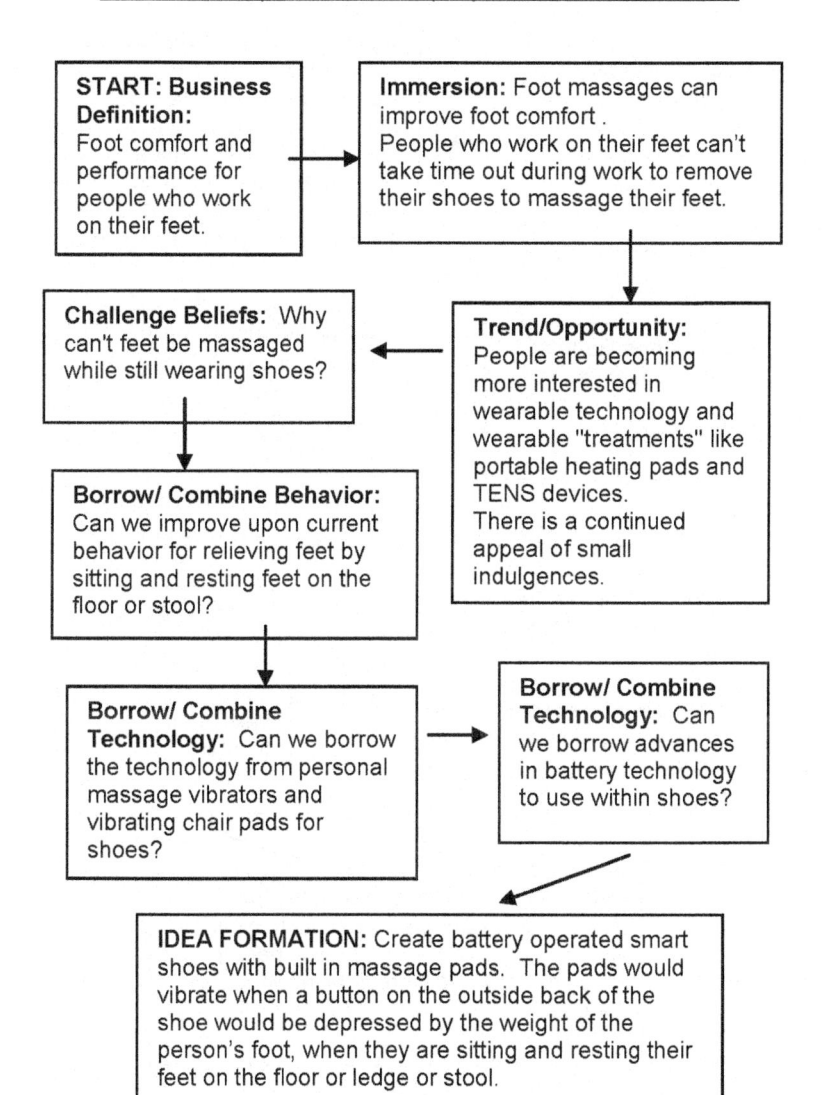

IDEA MAPPING (Foot Products 2)
Foot comfort & performance for people who work on their feet

START: Business Definition: Foot comfort and performance for people who work on their feet.

Immersion: Foot massages can improve foot comfort. People who work on their feet can't take time out during work to remove their shoes to massage their feet.

Challenge Beliefs: Why can't feet be massaged while still wearing shoes?

Trend/Opportunity: People are becoming more interested in wearable technology and wearable "treatments" like portable heating pads and TENS devices. There is a continued appeal of small indulgences.

Borrow/ Combine Behavior: Can we improve upon current behavior for relieving feet by sitting and resting feet on the floor or stool?

Borrow/ Combine Technology: Can we borrow the technology from personal massage vibrators and vibrating chair pads for shoes?

Borrow/ Combine Technology: Can we borrow advances in battery technology to use within shoes?

IDEA FORMATION: Create battery operated smart shoes with built in massage pads. The pads would vibrate when a button on the outside back of the shoe would be depressed by the weight of the person's foot, when they are sitting and resting their feet on the floor or ledge or stool.

◄ SEARCHING OUTSIDE THE WHITE BOX FOR NEW PRODUCT INNOVATION

IDEA MAPPING (Foot Products 3)
Foot comfort & performance for people who work on their feet

START: Business Definition: Foot comfort and performance for people who work on their feet.

Immersion: There are situations today where devices are used to reduce the weight and discomfort born by the feet, including braces and exoskeletons.

Challenge Beliefs: Why do feet have to bear the full weight of the person?

Trend/Opportunity: People are becoming more interested in wearable technology and wearable "treatments" like portable heating pads and TENS devices.

Borrow/ Combine Technology: Can we borrow the technology of exoskeletons as now being introduced in the military and industrial applications designed to augment the human body and its capabilities?

Mind Tools: Can we make exoskeletons lighter, more flexible, and thinner?

IDEA FORMATION: Create consumer friendly exoskeletons for people to wear in the form of enhanced garments, perhaps as slacks, that would reduce the weight on their feet.

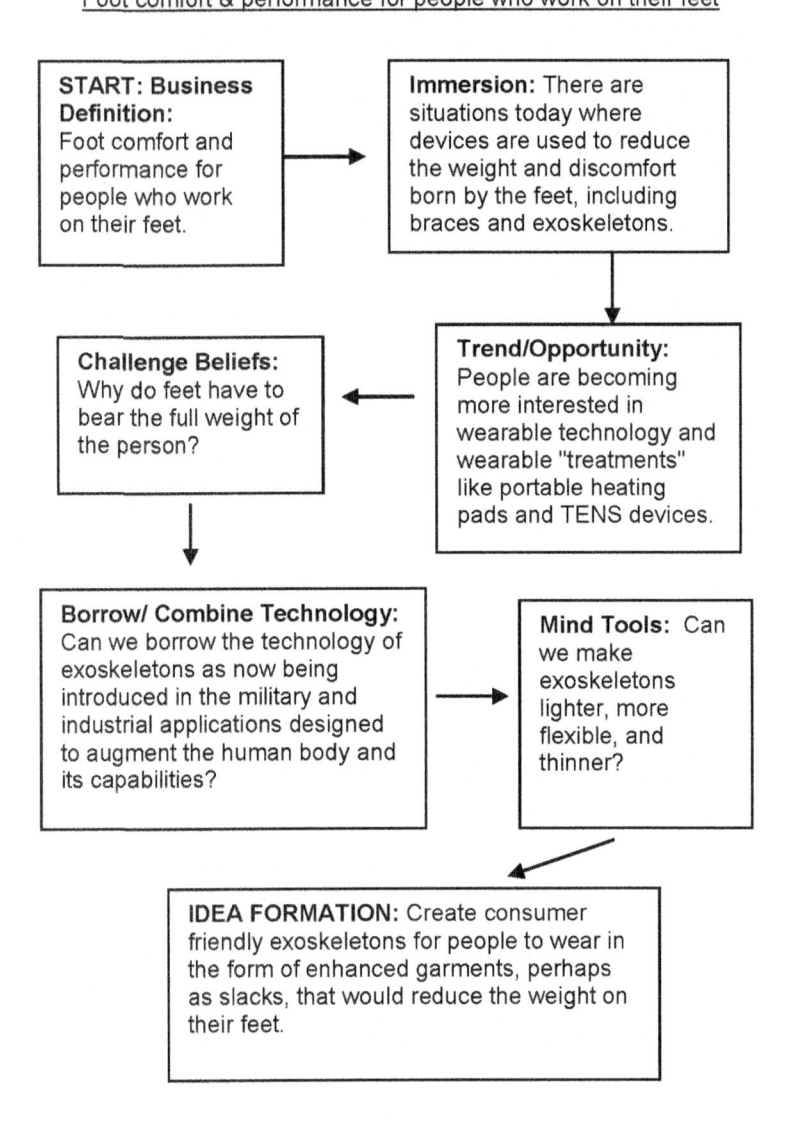

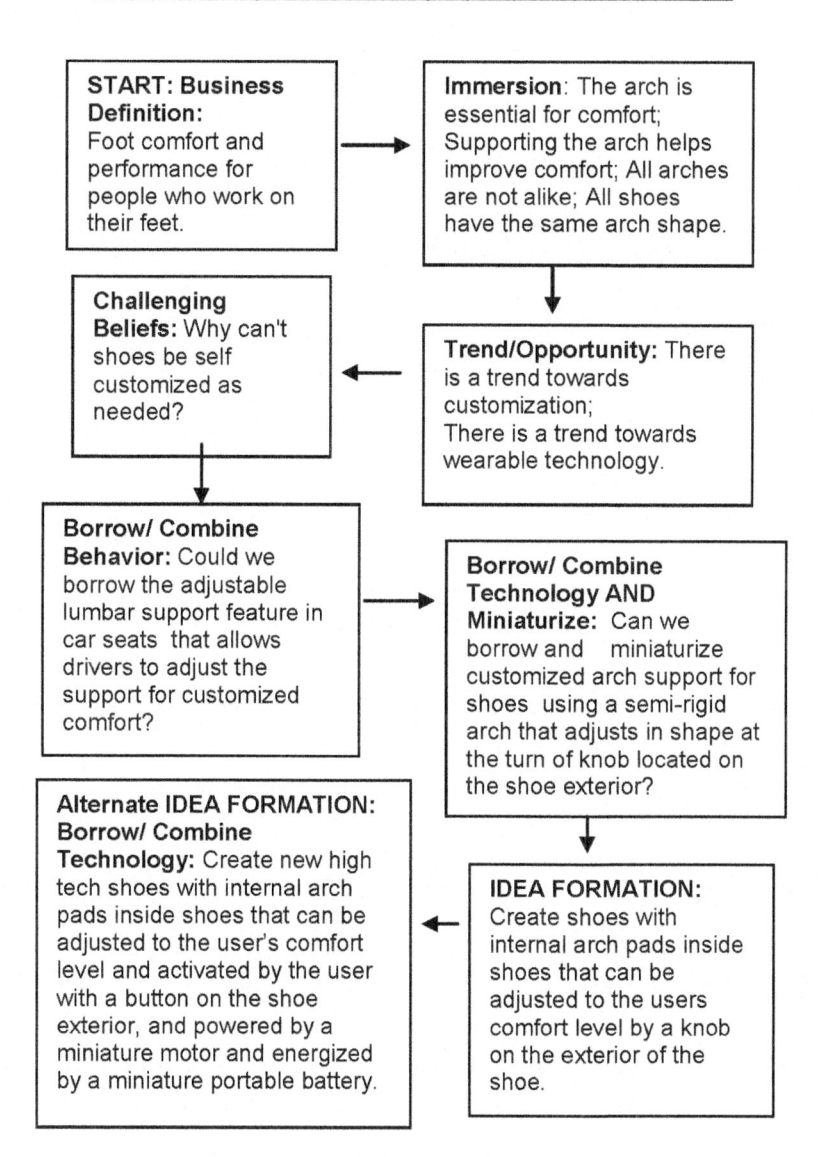

VISION DRIVING APPLICATIONS - FOOT PRODUCTS

IDEA MAPPING (Foot Products 4)
Foot comfort & performance for people who work on their feet

START: Business Definition: Foot comfort and performance for people who work on their feet.

Immersion: The arch is essential for comfort; Supporting the arch helps improve comfort; All arches are not alike; All shoes have the same arch shape.

Challenging Beliefs: Why can't shoes be self customized as needed?

Trend/Opportunity: There is a trend towards customization; There is a trend towards wearable technology.

Borrow/ Combine Behavior: Could we borrow the adjustable lumbar support feature in car seats that allows drivers to adjust the support for customized comfort?

Borrow/ Combine Technology AND Miniaturize: Can we borrow and miniaturize customized arch support for shoes using a semi-rigid arch that adjusts in shape at the turn of knob located on the shoe exterior?

Alternate IDEA FORMATION: Borrow/ Combine Technology: Create new high tech shoes with internal arch pads inside shoes that can be adjusted to the user's comfort level and activated by the user with a button on the shoe exterior, and powered by a miniature motor and energized by a miniature portable battery.

IDEA FORMATION: Create shoes with internal arch pads inside shoes that can be adjusted to the users comfort level by a knob on the exterior of the shoe.

CHAPTER **18**

Vision Driving Applications - Sun Protection

In this chapter we focus on a new business arena, products that protect people from the harmful effects of the sun.

Let's start with a broad **Business Definition**: Products or services that protect us from the sun, sold to all consumers in retail or on-line venues, and manufactured by contract manufacturers. So far our definition makes no mention of constraints such as product form, how used, where used, etc. For now this is intended so that we are not yet restricted in where this will take us. If we were in the OTC Drug business we might want to add this dimension to our definition, but by doing so, we might never come up with a non-OTC Drug approach. But then again, if our competitors did not place this restriction on their business, they might pursue a viable alternative and end up threatening our (comfortable, familiar, and profitable) OTC Drug business. Also, in this definition we have not yet mentioned what we are protecting, whether it is the skin, eyes, head, body fatigue, etc.

For this exercise we want to be pro-active in building our business for the broadly defined need for providing sun protection *for skin*, and by *whatever means*. The protection we offer can satisfy several of the

VISION DRIVING APPLICATIONS - SUN PROTECTION

needs on the Maslow Need Hierarchy regarding **Safety** (skin safety, skin cancer prevention), **Belongingness** (where good looking healthy skin helps maintain relationships), and **Esteem** (the cosmetic benefits of good looking skin as a factor in maintaining our status).

So, for now, our business definition is: providing sun protection *for skin*, and by *whatever means,* and sold to all consumers in retail or on-line venues, and manufactured by contract manufacturers.

Next, we **Immerse** ourselves in the arena. What are the prevailing means of sun protection? The obvious list includes, sun visors, hats, any clothing, sun umbrellas, OTC Drug creams, lotions, liquids, and sprays. What are the effectiveness and limitations of each approach?

What we learn from this analysis is that each existing method has strengths and weaknesses. The sun umbrella is suitable for the beach but not for everyday use. And, once implanted in the sand or by an outdoor table, its position must be manually changed as the sun's position changes throughout the day. Clothing items are basically an all or nothing form of protection. Wear a shirt and you fully protect the skin, but you don't get the chance to tone your skin to a more attractive skin color. A sun skin protecting spray or lotion must be applied with forethought, and takes time, but allows for some skin toning. But, these forms lose some of their protection as the day wears on.

So, what is the optimum product? That answer depends on the use situation. To a construction worker, full clothing protection may be what is needed. To a young woman sunbather clothing is not an option. To the person who just goes about their business or pleasure in the open outdoors the ideal product may be something that provides continuous protection but without much required forethought.

In **Trending Analysis**, the observations and general opportunities we highlighted before will remain the same for this exercise as all others.

◄ SEARCHING OUTSIDE THE WHITE BOX FOR NEW PRODUCT INNOVATION

What will be different here is that we will see where these general opportunities can drive specific opportunities in our chosen business arena. A few of the most intriguing trends to consider here include the growing concern for skin damage from the reduction in the ozone layer, use of wearable's, and the application of smart technology to just about anything. The merits of these will be revealed in the Idea Mapping exercise.

Let's start by **Challenging the Belief** that any form of sun protection must be administered outside the body, via a cream or lotion or spray or garments or umbrellas, etc. What if we can alter the skin's cells on a temporary basis to increase its protection from harm, and administered via an ingestible pill? Also, why must we believe that skin protecting lotions or sprays lose effectiveness throughout the day? Why can't they increase their protecting ability in reaction to increasing sun exposure?

When we think of **Borrowing Behavior** we have a rich source of perspectives for our skin sun protection need arena. Where else is the idea of protection a factor? What can we learn and or borrow? What is protection? Protection can take many forms. A lightning rod attached to the upper part of a house is intended to attract lightning and then deflect its energy safely into the ground. An umbrella is held above our heads to protect us from getting wet. We take a flu shot to protect us from getting the flu. We have air bags in the car to activate on impact so we are not hurt by the force. People who work in nuclear power plants wear a radiation badge that measures exposure and reveals when that exposure becomes harmful, so that the person can leave the space. Transition® focal lenses change color to protect the eyes from sun glare.

When we look at nature, we can find another rich source of protection. How does nature protect? Tree bark protects the tree's pulp. An octopus spews out a black ink to hide from its enemies. A skunk protects itself by forcing horrible odors onto its enemies. Elephants

VISION DRIVING APPLICATIONS - SUN PROTECTION

protect their skin in the sun by using their trunks to douse themselves with sand dust.

From just these few examples, we can see that protection can be obvious, visible, or not, it can be pre-planned or it can become part of the event. It can be "administered" in advance to prevent the harmful event from occurring. It can alert us to harm so we can leave, or it can be integrated into our routine to insulate us from the effects of the event if and when it occurs. From the world of nature, we see that protection can be part of the entity itself (tree bark or turtle's shell), or it can be thrust outwards when needed to defend against an attack. It can be voluntary or involuntary, temporary or permanent.

So how can these behaviors help us in our skin sun protection challenge? What could we borrow or combine? In the Vision Driving process, this technique is part of the series of stimuli that drive the creation of disruptive new product ideas.

There is also a rich source of perspectives to consider when we look to **Borrowing Technology**. Can we borrow the idea of chemical transitions in the presence of light (such as Transition Lenses) for skin protection, to possibly increase the skin sun protecting ability of lotions or sprays as the sun's exposure increases? Another thing to consider is the growing use of technology wearables. It's both a driving trend and a source for imagining applications to skin sun protection. And, when I think of the sun and nature's technology, I think of both photosynthesis and heliotropism behavior. Can either of these have application to our task?

We have already touched on some **Mind Tools** for this exercise by challenging the belief that sun skin protection had to be administered outside the body. This conjured up the thought of skin sun protection as a lotion in a pill, ie as an ingestible pill. I expect that other such thoughts will reveal themselves in the Idea Mapping exercise.

IDEA MAPPING (Sun 1)
Products that provide people with skin sun protection

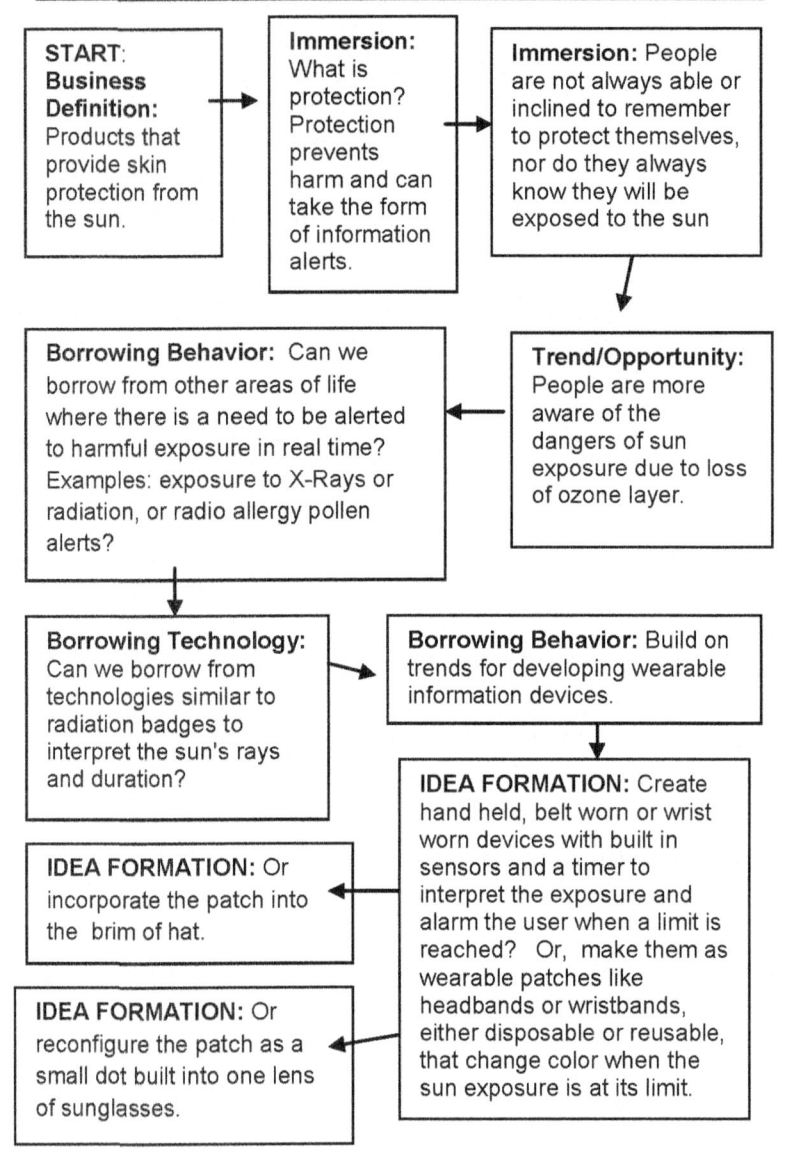

START: Business Definition: Products that provide skin protection from the sun.

Immersion: What is protection? Protection prevents harm and can take the form of information alerts.

Immersion: People are not always able or inclined to remember to protect themselves, nor do they always know they will be exposed to the sun

Borrowing Behavior: Can we borrow from other areas of life where there is a need to be alerted to harmful exposure in real time? Examples: exposure to X-Rays or radiation, or radio allergy pollen alerts?

Trend/Opportunity: People are more aware of the dangers of sun exposure due to loss of ozone layer.

Borrowing Technology: Can we borrow from technologies similar to radiation badges to interpret the sun's rays and duration?

Borrowing Behavior: Build on trends for developing wearable information devices.

IDEA FORMATION: Or incorporate the patch into the brim of hat.

IDEA FORMATION: Create hand held, belt worn or wrist worn devices with built in sensors and a timer to interpret the exposure and alarm the user when a limit is reached? Or, make them as wearable patches like headbands or wristbands, either disposable or reusable, that change color when the sun exposure is at its limit.

IDEA FORMATION: Or reconfigure the patch as a small dot built into one lens of sunglasses.

VISION DRIVING APPLICATIONS - SUN PROTECTION

IDEA MAPPING (Sun 2)
Products that provide people with skin sun protection

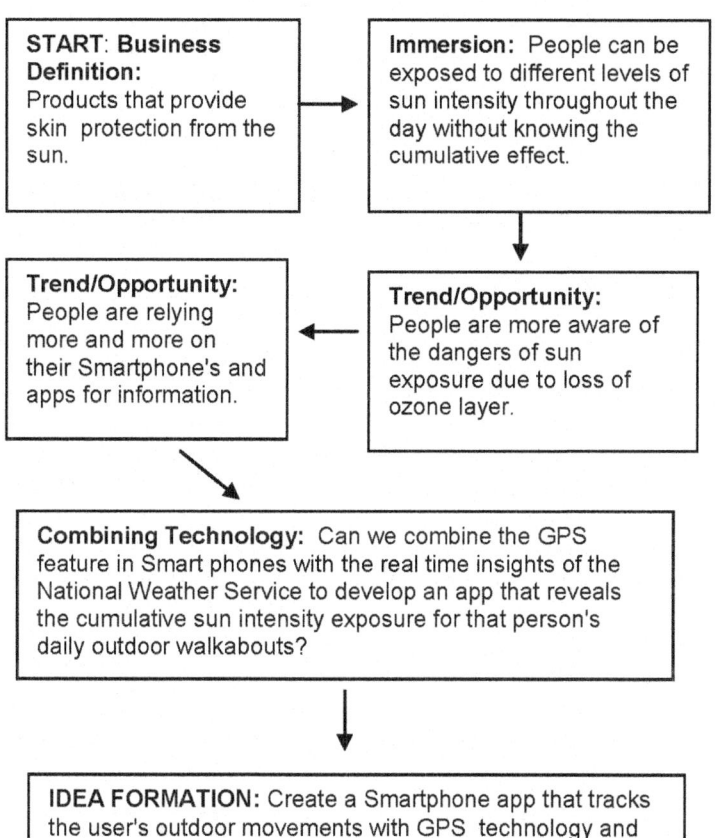

START: Business Definition: Products that provide skin protection from the sun.

Immersion: People can be exposed to different levels of sun intensity throughout the day without knowing the cumulative effect.

Trend/Opportunity: People are relying more and more on their Smartphone's and apps for information.

Trend/Opportunity: People are more aware of the dangers of sun exposure due to loss of ozone layer.

Combining Technology: Can we combine the GPS feature in Smart phones with the real time insights of the National Weather Service to develop an app that reveals the cumulative sun intensity exposure for that person's daily outdoor walkabouts?

IDEA FORMATION: Create a Smartphone app that tracks the user's outdoor movements with GPS technology and combines that with cumulative sunlight intensity data from the National Weather Service to provide a real time figure to the user for his/her sun exposure. When the limit is dangerous, it will sound a beep.

◄ SEARCHING OUTSIDE THE WHITE BOX FOR NEW PRODUCT INNOVATION

IDEA MAPPING (Sun 3)
Products that provide people with skin sun protection

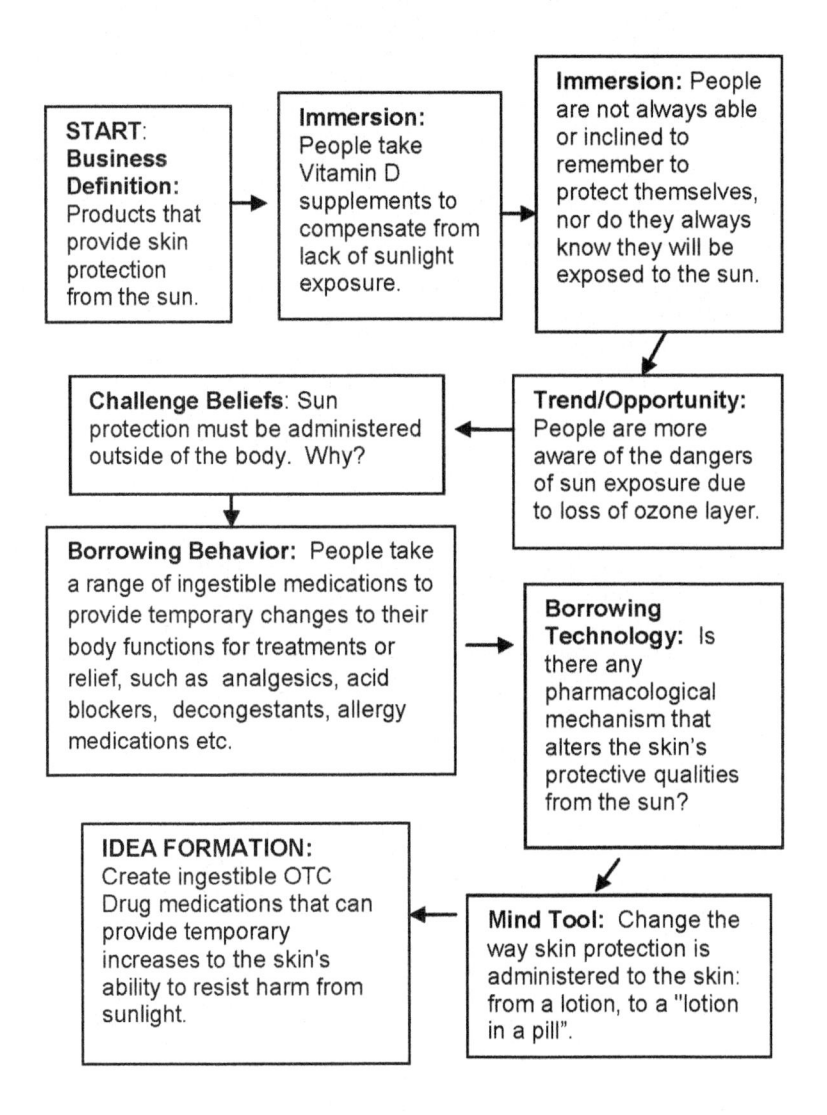

START: Business Definition: Products that provide skin protection from the sun.

Immersion: People take Vitamin D supplements to compensate from lack of sunlight exposure.

Immersion: People are not always able or inclined to remember to protect themselves, nor do they always know they will be exposed to the sun.

Challenge Beliefs: Sun protection must be administered outside of the body. Why?

Trend/Opportunity: People are more aware of the dangers of sun exposure due to loss of ozone layer.

Borrowing Behavior: People take a range of ingestible medications to provide temporary changes to their body functions for treatments or relief, such as analgesics, acid blockers, decongestants, allergy medications etc.

Borrowing Technology: Is there any pharmacological mechanism that alters the skin's protective qualities from the sun?

IDEA FORMATION: Create ingestible OTC Drug medications that can provide temporary increases to the skin's ability to resist harm from sunlight.

Mind Tool: Change the way skin protection is administered to the skin: from a lotion, to a "lotion in a pill".

VISION DRIVING APPLICATIONS - SUN PROTECTION

IDEA MAPPING (Sun 4)
Products that provide people with skin sun protection

This example reveals an NPD ideation that goes beyond the agreed to business definition in regard to how our skin sun protection products or services are manufactured and/or provided to the consumer. In this case the service is provided by a local business or municipal entity directly to the consumer. Although not within our business definition, it is a good example of how there may always be solutions beyond your business definition, and how Vision Driving could drive such ideation. Opportunities and threats to a business can come from anywhere. Here, the new service could be both an opportunity and threat for those in the skin sun protection business.

START: Business Definition: Products that provide skin protection from the sun.

Immersion: There is a world of information made available to consumers in the public space, such as time, temperature, bus arrival times, etc.

Trend/Opportunity: People are more aware of the dangers of sun exposure due to loss of ozone layer.

Immersion: In special outdoor locations where there is sun and water, we might see beach flags for surf conditions, and we might see temperature boards for beaches and pools.

Trend/Opportunity: We see more and more public surveillance and information gathering devices

Combining Technology: Can we combine solar sensors with public information gathering devices that would compute the sun's intensity to derive a "safe time in the sun" figure in minutes for public display?

IDEA FORMATION: Create a series of public information displays in public places, especially in sunny climates and especially at beaches, pools, and golf courses, that would continuously display the computed "safe time in the sun" figure in minutes for all people to see, so that they could take remedial actions as necessary.

CHAPTER **19**

Vision Driving Applications – Home Interior Air/Ambiance Conditioning

As always, our starting point is with the **Business Definition.** We are in the business of improving the home interior air or ambience to improve the quality of life at home. We provide products of all types, without restrictions of form or technology, which are sold to consumers via retail outlets and on-line venues. We have the means to source our products from any viable manufacturer. We are specifically not including home security in this arena.

This is a broad definition for a fictional company that has the courage to see their business in a much larger sense than some of the actual companies in the business segments as represented by the current range of products. Today these would include companies that market fans, air-conditioners, air fresheners, sound machines, lighting products, portable heaters, wall insulation, even light bulbs and lava machines. Our definition is intended to make this exercise exciting. In the real world, many of these companies could expand their business definitions in a range of different pathways to exploit some of these new growth arenas.

VISION DRIVING APPLICATIONS – HOME INTERIOR AIR/AMBIANCE CONDITIONING ⌇

When we **Immerse** ourselves in this business we have a lot of ground to cover. What is the current range of products available and what is the current range of needs satisfied by these products? How do needs change by virtue of demographics, geography, time of day, room to room, season, number of individuals in the room, a person's health, etc? What we will learn is that this is a complex arena, with many variables and factors that come into play as we seek to improve our interior air and ambience quality. Our needs in a city apartment may be different than that in a rural setting. A child's room may have different needs than that of their parents. A bathroom has different demands than a bedroom. Our needs change when we sleep vs when we have a house party.

Another huge source of information comes from our understanding of how various ambient factors will affect us. These might include air quality, lighting, sound, smell, temperature, humidity, colors, and others. And in a larger sense, we might want to see how companionship becomes a factor in the ambiance within a home. This will be a deep study.

With **Trending Analysis** we want to re-visit our list of general opportunities and ask if any can have bearing on the Vision Driving task. The most obvious ones to consider are applications of smart technologies to all home appliances, customizations and personalization, continued concerns for germs within and outside our homes, and interest in aromatherapy.

To think about **Challenging Beliefs** we have to open our minds beyond what we have come to expect about our home interiors. We can control the amount of light that enters our home. Why can't we prevent noise from entering our home? We think about air purifiers that remove pollutants from our home. What can we add to our interior air to improve our health or well-being? Why can't we make the home smart enough to know what to do if ever "assaulted" by incoming allergens, germs, pollutants, etc, without our intervention? Why must we rely on manufacturers to determine which scents to make available to us for store bought air fresheners?

When we think of **Borrowing or Combining Behavior** we can look at any type of interior, in any economic activity, where the interior space is altered to suit the daily needs. A music recording studio needs sound management, a drug manufacturing facility needs to be sterile or close to sterile, a greenhouse needs clear windows to let the sunlight in, a bathroom or kitchen typically need exhaust fans, etc. We won't know what has application to our Vision Driving exercise until we get underway.

For **Borrowing or Combining Technology** we have a lot to look at. What technologies exist today that have some bearing on interior air or ambience. From our Immersion exercise we are already familiar with room air fresheners, air conditioners, heaters, sound machines, air purifiers, and more recently, devices that create white light for those who suffer from winter seasonal light deprivation.

Recently we are seeing the emergence of devices that produce negative ions inside a home that are able to improve people's health and well being. There are now studies that show that negative ions, which are oxygen atoms charged with an extra electron, are able to clear the air in a home of allergens, mold, bacteria and viruses. Where do we experience this negative ion effect today? At the beach or after a rainfall we are already smelling the negative ions, and possibly even receiving the healthful benefits without knowing it. That is big news. How can borrow this in our Vision Driving exercise?

Another recent development to consider is the creation of artificial photosynthesis on a membrane. Julian Melchiorri, a Royal College of Art Graduate has developed an artificial leaf that can mimic the function of photosynthesis. Here, a new chemistry system impregnated

VISION DRIVING APPLICATIONS – HOME INTERIOR AIR/AMBIANCE CONDITIONING

onto a membrane is able to absorb carbon dioxide, water, and sunlight and then via a chemical reaction, produce and release fresh oxygen into the environment. There are already great thinkers who are considering how this will improve space exploration. Our question is: Does this have applications in home interiors?

We can find other technologies to think about. If we can quickly customize our lighting in a room, is there a way to use technology to quickly customize the scents in a room? Can we look to the industrial sectors where sound and noise mitigation is a factor, and apply these technologies to reducing noise entering a home? The air force uses stealth technology to deflect radar. Can we employ sound deflection technology to reduce noise entering the home?

Using **Mind Tools** can be fun here. There are a lot of people who live in big cities who currently use ear plugs when they go to sleep. If you are in any drug store in New York City you will find an enormous supply of different types and brands of ear plugs. Why can't we take the idea of ear plugs and make them enormous....to the size of a bedroom to keep noise out? And, if home color ink jet printers can use 6 color ink wells to customize a full spectrum for printed photos, is there a way to use the same phenomena to customize in home air freshening? This should get us thinking.

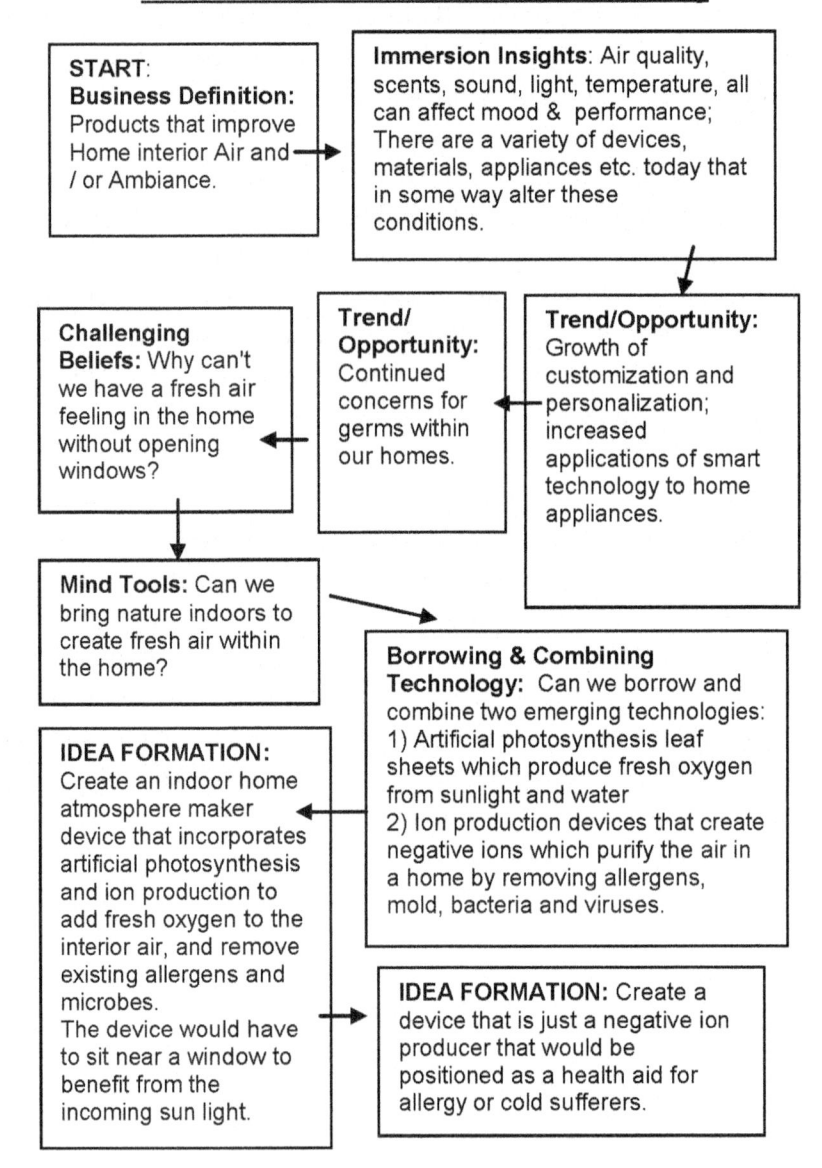

◄ SEARCHING OUTSIDE THE WHITE BOX FOR NEW PRODUCT INNOVATION

IDEA MAPPING (Home 1)
Home Interior Air/Ambiance Conditioning

START:
Business Definition: Products that improve Home interior Air and / or Ambiance.

Immersion Insights: Air quality, scents, sound, light, temperature, all can affect mood & performance; There are a variety of devices, materials, appliances etc. today that in some way alter these conditions.

Challenging Beliefs: Why can't we have a fresh air feeling in the home without opening windows?

Trend/ Opportunity: Continued concerns for germs within our homes.

Trend/Opportunity: Growth of customization and personalization; increased applications of smart technology to home appliances.

Mind Tools: Can we bring nature indoors to create fresh air within the home?

Borrowing & Combining Technology: Can we borrow and combine two emerging technologies:
1) Artificial photosynthesis leaf sheets which produce fresh oxygen from sunlight and water
2) Ion production devices that create negative ions which purify the air in a home by removing allergens, mold, bacteria and viruses.

IDEA FORMATION: Create an indoor home atmosphere maker device that incorporates artificial photosynthesis and ion production to add fresh oxygen to the interior air, and remove existing allergens and microbes.
The device would have to sit near a window to benefit from the incoming sun light.

IDEA FORMATION: Create a device that is just a negative ion producer that would be positioned as a health aid for allergy or cold sufferers.

◄ 190

VISION DRIVING APPLICATIONS – HOME INTERIOR AIR/AMBIANCE CONDITIONING

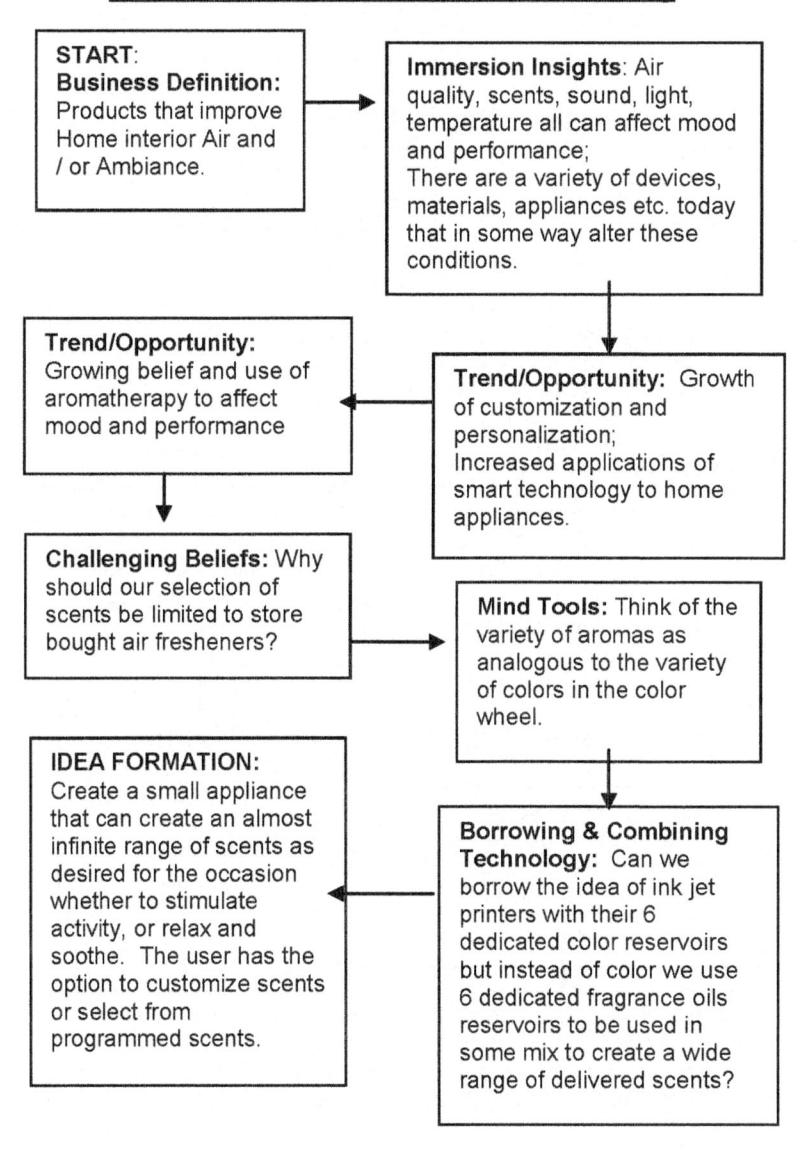

IDEA MAPPING (Home 2)
Home Interior Air/Ambiance Conditioning

START:
Business Definition: Products that improve Home interior Air and / or Ambiance.

Immersion Insights: Air quality, scents, sound, light, temperature all can affect mood and performance;
There are a variety of devices, materials, appliances etc. today that in some way alter these conditions.

Trend/Opportunity: Growing belief and use of aromatherapy to affect mood and performance

Trend/Opportunity: Growth of customization and personalization;
Increased applications of smart technology to home appliances.

Challenging Beliefs: Why should our selection of scents be limited to store bought air fresheners?

Mind Tools: Think of the variety of aromas as analogous to the variety of colors in the color wheel.

IDEA FORMATION: Create a small appliance that can create an almost infinite range of scents as desired for the occasion whether to stimulate activity, or relax and soothe. The user has the option to customize scents or select from programmed scents.

Borrowing & Combining Technology: Can we borrow the idea of ink jet printers with their 6 dedicated color reservoirs but instead of color we use 6 dedicated fragrance oils reservoirs to be used in some mix to create a wide range of delivered scents?

◄ SEARCHING OUTSIDE THE WHITE BOX FOR NEW PRODUCT INNOVATION

IDEA MAPPING (Home 3)
Home Interior Air/Ambiance Conditioning

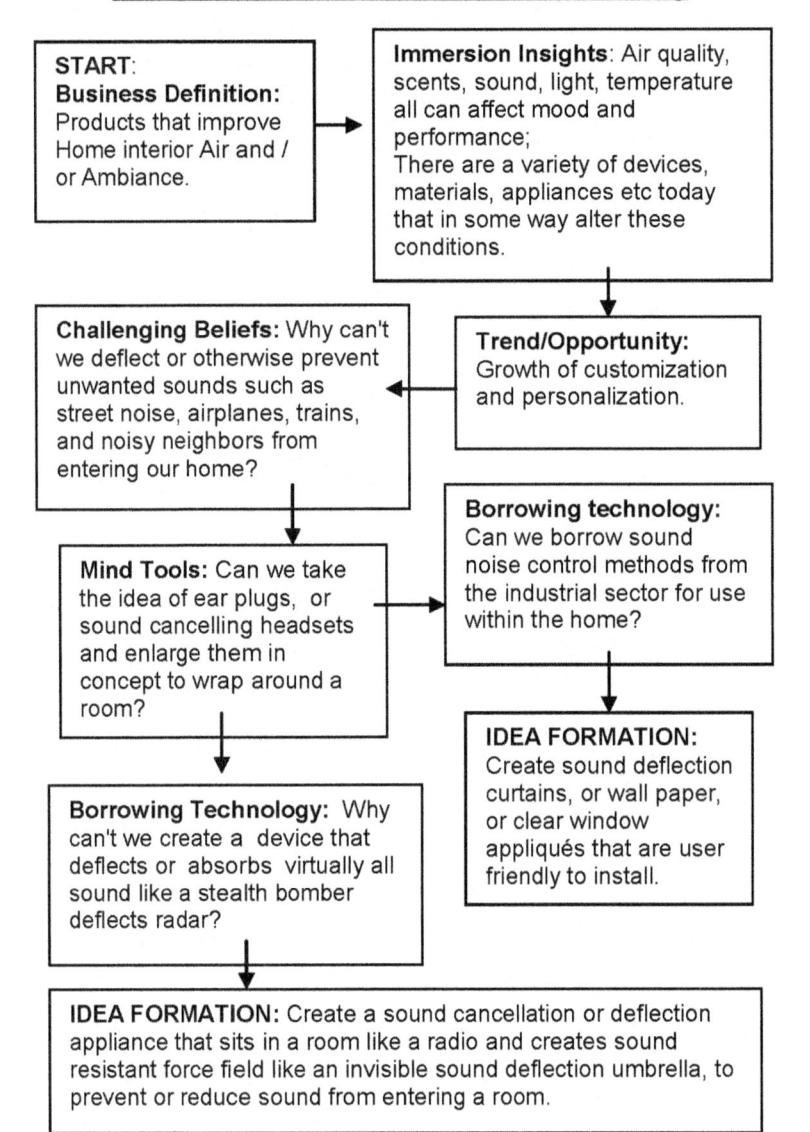

START:
Business Definition: Products that improve Home interior Air and / or Ambiance.

Immersion Insights: Air quality, scents, sound, light, temperature all can affect mood and performance; There are a variety of devices, materials, appliances etc today that in some way alter these conditions.

Challenging Beliefs: Why can't we deflect or otherwise prevent unwanted sounds such as street noise, airplanes, trains, and noisy neighbors from entering our home?

Trend/Opportunity: Growth of customization and personalization.

Mind Tools: Can we take the idea of ear plugs, or sound cancelling headsets and enlarge them in concept to wrap around a room?

Borrowing technology: Can we borrow sound noise control methods from the industrial sector for use within the home?

Borrowing Technology: Why can't we create a device that deflects or absorbs virtually all sound like a stealth bomber deflects radar?

IDEA FORMATION: Create sound deflection curtains, or wall paper, or clear window appliqués that are user friendly to install.

IDEA FORMATION: Create a sound cancellation or deflection appliance that sits in a room like a radio and creates sound resistant force field like an invisible sound deflection umbrella, to prevent or reduce sound from entering a room.

CHAPTER **20**

Vision Driving Applications – Value Added Wipes

This is a different type of business arena than our previous examples. In this example I want to demonstrate how the Vision Driving process can work for a product form arena, not a specific consumer need arena.

Wipes have been around for quite some time, and currently take on many different configurations and applications, from wet naps, to alcohol swabs, denture cleaning wipes, teeth whitening strips, surface cleaning wipes, baby wipes, industrial applications, etc.

Let's start by **Defining the Business**, touching on the 5 elements that we detailed earlier.

Let's assume that our business today provides users with a disposable liquid impregnated flexible paper like substrate that is used to clean and possibly disinfect surfaces in a range of settings. These may include hospitals, homes, and businesses of all types, Doctor's offices, and just about any place where a convenient disposable cleaning wipe is needed. We manufacture the wipes in our own facilities using

SEARCHING OUTSIDE THE WHITE BOX FOR NEW PRODUCT INNOVATION

high speed equipment, and distribute the finished products via master distributors to a wide range of end users.

We can maintain this business definition or expand it. If our management is content with this business and its growth potential, then we may choose to stay with this definition. Our position and share within the industry may already be strong and growing, without the need to extend beyond what we now find to be a comfortable competitive position. We may want to continue our strategies of improving our existing products, with new product textures, thicknesses, or sizes, and the types of cleaning chemicals impregnated for different cleaning tasks. We may want to improve our packaging to add more convenient dispensing, and improved shelf life to our wipes. And we may want to continue to grow our distribution opportunities. NPD has its place within this business definition, and the Vision Driving process can be applied.

But if we are not satisfied with our cleaning wipes business with its current position and growth potential, and if we see the limitations within this mature business, then we would be well served to expand our current business definition. It is ironic, but quite possible that two very different companies in this form arena may want to seek disruptive NPD ideas. One company may be the leader in the industry and wants to expand that position, while another company may be in an untenable position with a small share and declining prospects, and in need of finding a growth path. For different reasons, it may make sense for each company to entertain expansions to their business definitions.

As we look at all 5 elements of the business definition we can see an enormous range of options, should we wish to expand our business.

1. What needs do we satisfy?

    Right now we provide cleaning.

VISION DRIVING APPLICATIONS – VALUE ADDED WIPES

What other needs could a wipe serve?

2. What product or service do we provide?

   Now we provide flexible, disposable, liquid impregnated cleaning wipes.

   Should we consider different forms?

   Should we consider creating new types of wipes by adding other dynamics to wipes to provide new benefits?

3. Who are our primary consumers or customers?

   Right now our target users are all potential users of cleaning products: consumers, industry, medical, etc.

   Should we focus on specific end users?

4. How shall we provide/distribute our product or service to them?

   We currently have a wide distribution network serving a range of consumer and commercial users.

   Should we consider other means of distribution?

   Should we expand? Should we focus?

5. How shall we configure our service or manufacture our product?

   Now we make our products using non woven substrates impregnated with a liquid on high speed equipment.

SEARCHING OUTSIDE THE WHITE BOX FOR NEW PRODUCT INNOVATION

How can we enhance our manufacture process to add other "mechanisms" to the substrate (eg chemistry, electronics, materials, etc) that add utility to our product or create entirely new utility?

Should we consider other substrates that can still run on our high speed equipment?

Our fictitious company sees itself today as in the cleaning wipes business. Linear expansion opportunities for this company would take them into new types of cleaning or polishing products. But when it comes to more aggressive expansion, given its huge capital investment in the high speed equipment used in the manufacturing of wipes, it sees itself first as a wipes company and second as a cleaning company. So, the question facing this company is: what different end benefits can be delivered to a user other than cleaning if we were to apply something other than cleaning chemicals to the wipes? That is a big question.

This company chooses to be bold in expanding its business definition to: A business that provides users with a disposable flexible paper like substrate that is used to either: a) alter a surface or environment, or b) provide some other benefit to the user, or c) provide knowledge about an environment. This last item, knowledge, is already a giveaway about how we can expand the range of benefits delivered by a wipe, ie by providing information, insight, or a diagnosis about the surface or environment. Continuing with our business definition..... the product is manufactured on our existing high speed equipment, perhaps with some modifications. We can leverage the company's wide distribution strength by thinking about a range of possible end users, but we decide to focus first on one group, consumers, as a start.

This definition would clearly open up an entirely new range of products that go well beyond providing users with the benefit of a convenient cleaning wipe. With this definition and a little imagination, we could deliver warmth, cold, sound, taste, light, or provide a substrate that absorbs moisture or airborne chemicals, or conversely that releases moisture or airborne chemicals, or a substrate that actually delivers energy when in use. We can also consider where a flexible substrate can provide protection to a surface from heat, cold, light, scratches, dirt, or other environmental or ambient assaults. And with our expanded definition now including information, our wipe can be imagined to reveal a host of information about the environment where it is placed, such as air quality, the presence of microbes, moisture level, temperature, etc.

As we see, just by expanding the business definition we are already on our way to imagining new disruptive NPD ideas. Unlike the earlier Vision Driving examples where we started with a need arena first (eg foot care, or sun protection, etc.) in this example we are starting first with a form arena with new wipe technologies, and then seeking ways that it can provide benefits that fulfill as yet unidentified needs. But what benefits do our new products provide? And which of these new NPD ideas are best for the company to pursue? Vision Driving in this new arena is going to be exciting for our fictitious company.

The next step in the Vision Driving process is **Immersion** in the arena. But how do we immerse ourselves in an arena that could include literally hundreds of usage scenarios and delivered benefits? This is tough, but the place to start is in the form itself. This type of immersion will help us in the Vision Driving process create NPD ideas that go well beyond the cleaning wipes segment.

First, look at any and all types of configurations that can take the shape of a thin flexible substrate that can be manufactured on high speed equipment. There is a world of manufactured consumer products with flexible substrates: window shades, toilet paper, paper towels, textiles, candy, pasta, etc. We must also immerse ourselves in all technologies that can be configured into a flexible substrate.

SEARCHING OUTSIDE THE WHITE BOX FOR NEW PRODUCT INNOVATION

There are many. A printed circuit board or electric conductive ribbons can be produced on a flexible strip. So can new batteries. There are diagnostic aids such as the thin strip used to diagnose chemicals in the urine stream as a pregnancy test, and flexible ribbons or strips that reveal temperature changes, and pH testing strips that change color in reaction to the range of acid or alkaline levels. There are even individually wrapped sterile ophthalmic strips used for detection of corneal abrasions and diagnosing Dry Eye Syndrome.

As in the other examples, the **Trending Analysis** starts with the list of general opportunities and then is re-visited to determine if the trends can drive specific opportunities for the arena in study, wipes. This study will be more involved and wide open than our previous examples where the need arena can help us focus on specific trends that may apply. Here, in this exercise, we would really need to pressure test every trend to see if it can make sense for our form arena.

For instance, there is a growing trend towards incorporating smart technology into just about everything...so what would a smart wipe be? What could it do? There is a growing trend in the use and applications of solar power. Can we apply solar cells to a flexible substrate for low power limited use requirements? The world is growing more hostile and dangerous from events that are man made and / or climate induced. People are becoming more concerned about food safety and disease prevention. How can a wipe or other flexible substrate meet any emerging needs from these trends?

How do we apply the next step, **Challenging Beliefs?** We can start by challenging the belief that wipes can only deliver a chemical liquid as impregnated into the substrate. In a sense we already set the stage for this thinking by broadening the business definition, and conducting our immersion exercise which has taken us well beyond the notion of delivering a liquid cleaning chemical to another surface

VISION DRIVING APPLICATIONS – VALUE ADDED WIPES

When we think about **Borrowing or Combining Behavior or Technology** we begin to envision other actions or dynamics that can be added to the flexible membrane (not necessarily a paper or non-woven substrate) to deliver a new benefit in use. It is not so far fetched to imagine that the new substrate can deliver air freshening, or grass seeds, or warmth (via exothermic reaction once exposed to the air), or a pollution tester that changes color in reaction to a chemical in the air once it is exposed, or provides on-demand energy, or provides information or a diagnosis, about the environment when exposed to specific stimuli.

There are many more possibilities when we look at emerging innovations that can be configured into thin and flexible substrates. With some imagination, we can come up with many exciting new technologies that can be borrowed or combined into our flexible substrates to create disruptive NPD ideas for our wipe company to consider. Some of these technologies include:

- Artificial photosynthesis on a membrane, a new chemistry technology developed by Julian Melchiorri that produces fresh oxygen when the membrane is exposed to carbon dioxide, sunlight and water. Can this chemistry system be applied to a wipe substrate?

- The second phenomenon, chemiluminescence, has been around for quite some time as chemical reactions that produce light without heat. We see this in nature as bioluminescence in such marine creatures as jellyfish, and octopi, and in insects like the lightning bugs. Now this phenomenon has been captured by science for portable on-demand use by man. Current applications include light sticks, bracelets, and other devices used for nighttime fun, or camping, or outdoor lighting. Can this be applied to a flexible wipe or strip? How would we use this?

◄ SEARCHING OUTSIDE THE WHITE BOX FOR NEW PRODUCT INNOVATION

- The third technology involves a chemistry mixture of iron powder, salt, moisture and activated carbon that produces an exothermic reaction that releases heat when exposed to the air. Common uses today include hand warmers for people who work or play outdoors in the cold. Can this chemistry be applied to a thin pouch?

- The fourth technology involves the use of diagnostic chemistry systems imbedded into pads or sticks for such things as pregnancy urine test kits that offer a yes or no indicator when the stick is exposed to specific chemicals in urine. Can any other chemistry systems be imbedded into substrate and offer new diagnostic information when exposed to air, or water, or to a surface, or skin, or the tongue, or saliva, and on?

- The next technology is aligned with the growing use of renewable energy, specifically the use of solar energy. New low cost solar cell receivers are being made of tiny silicon beads bonded into an aluminum foil substrate that captures light and converts it into electrical energy. The flexibility of this configuration makes it ideal for special applications. Does this have application to our wipes company?

- The final technology on this quick list of mine involves the growing improvements and use of thin flexible batteries, now available in a variety of shapes, sizes, and capacity. Can this technology be imbedded into a flexible substrate for on demand use? Can the combination of flexible batteries and flexible solar cells have special use?

In this example, we're going to allow the Vision Driving process to reveal where and how any **Mind Tools** can help drive our NPD ideation.

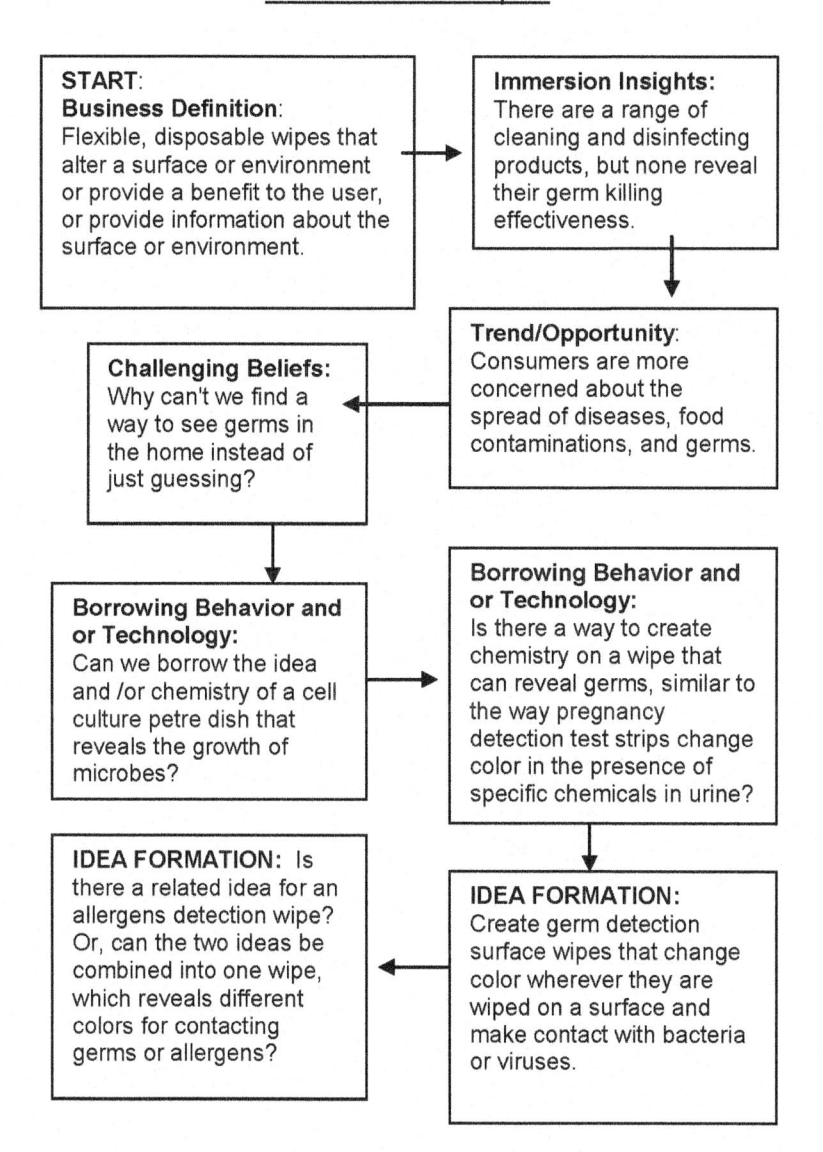

IDEA MAPPING (Wipes 1)
Value Added Wipes

START:
Business Definition:
Flexible, disposable wipes that alter a surface or environment or provide a benefit to the user, or provide information about the surface or environment.

Immersion Insights:
There are a range of cleaning and disinfecting products, but none reveal their germ killing effectiveness.

Trend/Opportunity:
Consumers are more concerned about the spread of diseases, food contaminations, and germs.

Challenging Beliefs:
Why can't we find a way to see germs in the home instead of just guessing?

Borrowing Behavior and or Technology:
Can we borrow the idea and /or chemistry of a cell culture petre dish that reveals the growth of microbes?

Borrowing Behavior and or Technology:
Is there a way to create chemistry on a wipe that can reveal germs, similar to the way pregnancy detection test strips change color in the presence of specific chemicals in urine?

IDEA FORMATION: Is there a related idea for an allergens detection wipe? Or, can the two ideas be combined into one wipe, which reveals different colors for contacting germs or allergens?

IDEA FORMATION:
Create germ detection surface wipes that change color wherever they are wiped on a surface and make contact with bacteria or viruses.

◄ SEARCHING OUTSIDE THE WHITE BOX FOR NEW PRODUCT INNOVATION

IDEA MAPPING (Wipes 2)
Value Added Wipes

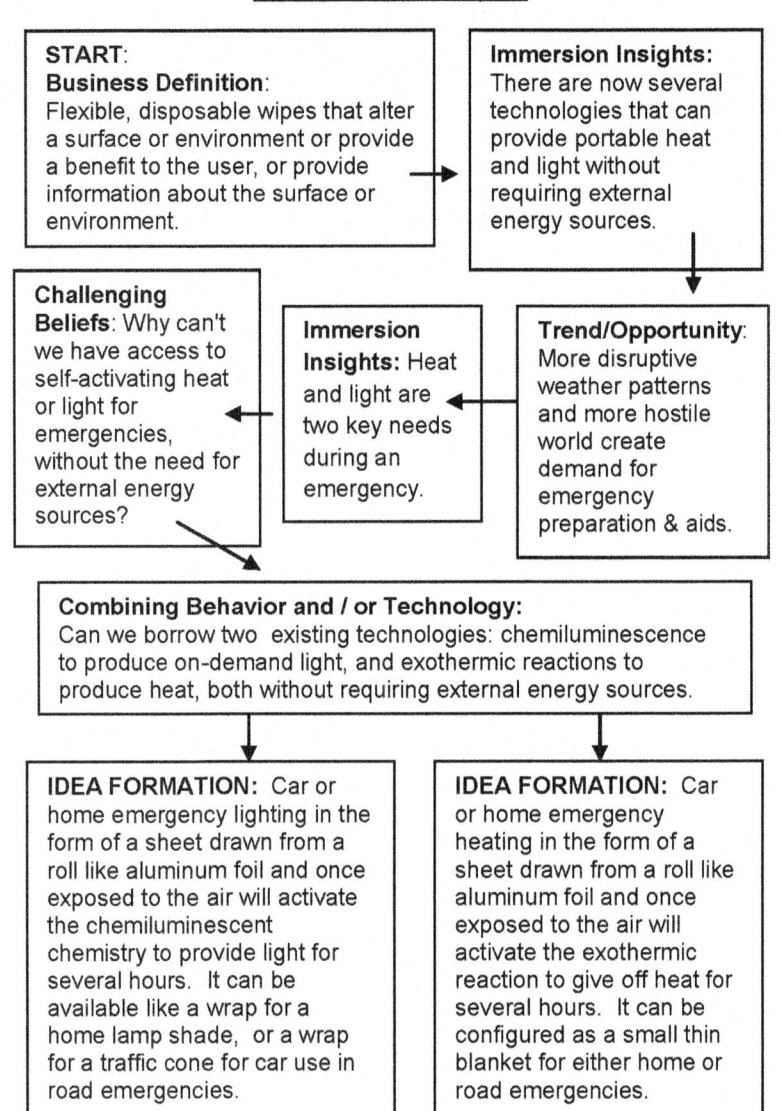

START:
Business Definition: Flexible, disposable wipes that alter a surface or environment or provide a benefit to the user, or provide information about the surface or environment.

Immersion Insights: There are now several technologies that can provide portable heat and light without requiring external energy sources.

Challenging Beliefs: Why can't we have access to self-activating heat or light for emergencies, without the need for external energy sources?

Immersion Insights: Heat and light are two key needs during an emergency.

Trend/Opportunity: More disruptive weather patterns and more hostile world create demand for emergency preparation & aids.

Combining Behavior and / or Technology: Can we borrow two existing technologies: chemiluminescence to produce on-demand light, and exothermic reactions to produce heat, both without requiring external energy sources.

IDEA FORMATION: Car or home emergency lighting in the form of a sheet drawn from a roll like aluminum foil and once exposed to the air will activate the chemiluminescent chemistry to provide light for several hours. It can be available like a wrap for a home lamp shade, or a wrap for a traffic cone for car use in road emergencies.

IDEA FORMATION: Car or home emergency heating in the form of a sheet drawn from a roll like aluminum foil and once exposed to the air will activate the exothermic reaction to give off heat for several hours. It can be configured as a small thin blanket for either home or road emergencies.

IDEA MAPPING (Wipes 3)
Value Added Wipes

START:
Business Definition: Flexible, disposable wipes that alter a surface or environment or provide a benefit to the user, or provide information about the surface or environment.

Immersion Insights: There is now a range of diagnostic test strips that use a flexible substrate and imbedded chemistry systems.

Combining Behavior and or Technology: Can we borrow the idea of pregnancy test strips and find the chemistry system technology that can change color when exposed to bad breadth?

Challenging Beliefs: Why can't we have a way to know when we have bad breadth instead of guessing or the embarrassment of asking people?

IDEA FORMATION: Create single use disposable sheets or tabs the size of a large postage stamp that is used to determine if bad breath is present. They could be dispensed similar to a roll of stamps. The person either blows on the strip or places the strip on their tongue. The strip changes colors when it detects the chemicals in bad breadth.

CHAPTER **21**

Vision Driving Applications - Food Storage & Protection

First we want to **Define our Business**, which for now will be products that help all people store and protect food and maintain its freshness inside the home, or while they are mobile or at work or play. Our products can take any form, are manufactured by outside contracted factories, and are sold to consumers in retail or on-line venues.

We are clearly creating a very expanded business definition in scope. The current segments within our defined arena are represented by such products as refrigerators, storage containers and storage bags, lunch boxes and portable coolers, backpacks, beverage thermoses, home wine coolers, food and drink vending machines, picnic baskets, bread boxes, cup holders in car interiors, food take-out containers and cups, and the military's MREs, *Meals Ready to Eat*. If we were in any of these businesses we might want to look beyond our current segment to consider what any business expansion would mean for us as an opportunity or threat. A Vision Driving exercise with this business definition will do this.

Next, we **Immerse** ourselves in the arena. What are the various conditions that food can be exposed to? What are the special

◀ 204

VISION DRIVING APPLICATIONS - FOOD STORAGE & PROTECTION ➤

needs at home, enroute, at work, in the car, or elsewhere? What is the current range of materials used to store and protect food? What are the current problems and or limitations of current products and methods? Finally, are there special needs for special people or functions? What are the food storage needs of hikers, beachgoers, boaters, campers, astronautics, office workers, police officers, school children, shut-ins, construction workers, seniors, etc? You get the idea.

There are ample general opportunities from our **Trending Analysis** to re-visit for this exercise. Some of the obvious ones include: growing concern for food contaminations, less trust in government to control the purity of our food supply, more 24/7 active lifestyles, retailers need for increasing revenue to offset losses to on-line venues, more people eating alone, growing appeal of customization, growing applications of smart technologies, etc.

When we think of **Challenging Beliefs** regarding food storage and protection, the first questions might include: Why can't consumers have their own means to keep foods contamination free instead of relying on others? Why can't we take all the functions that a kitchen affords in storing foods with us by using portable power sources? Why can't we extend the shelf life of food? Right now we store food in a variety of places such as pantry, counter top, bread box, refrigerator, freezer, wine cooler, etc. Why do we need all of these? Why can't we have one intelligent storage device that knows the right storage conditions for each item, and then provides that condition?

Without much thinking, there is a lot to consider for **Borrowing and /or Combining Behavior or Technologies.** Can we borrow portable energy sources to help store food on-the-go? How can smart technologies improve upon current food storage methods? Can we look at other environments where food is made or cleansed for

SEARCHING OUTSIDE THE WHITE BOX FOR NEW PRODUCT INNOVATION

application to the home? What can we borrow from such processes as food sterilization, or vacuum packing, or freeze drying etc? And, just to make things interesting, we can pressure test some far out things for consideration, like voice controlled systems, or proximity sensors, or temperature indicator strips, and portable exothermic and endothermic reactions that respectively produce portable heat or cold. As with all Vision Driving exercises, a world view of outside technologies and their possible application to the task at hand, is always an exciting step.

Some of the **Mind Tools** that may play into this task might include: miniaturization, configuring unrelated items, and the idea of imagining what various factory processes might look like in the home.

VISION DRIVING APPLICATIONS - FOOD STORAGE & PROTECTION

IDEA MAPPING (Food Storage 1)
Food Storage & Protection

START: Business Definition: Products that help store & protect food at home and on the go.

Immersion: Consumers are more aware of food contents and origins.

Trend/Opportunity: Growing incidence of food contaminations are creating more consumer concerns for food quality and safety.

Trend/Opportunity: Decreasing trust in government's ability to protect our food supply.

Challenge Beliefs: Why must consumers rely on others to keep our food supply free of "bugs"?

Borrow Technology: What types of food sterilization technology can we borrow from industry and apply in other settings?

Mind Tools: Can we modify a factory food sterilization process and make it smaller?

Trend/Opportunity: Retailers are losing business to on-line retailers and need new sources of revenue.

IDEA FORMATION: Create an in-home microwave like appliance that will sterilize our food without altering it.

IDEA FORMATION: Create food sterilization services within retail grocery stores to provide a new service for consumers and create a new source of revenue for retailers.

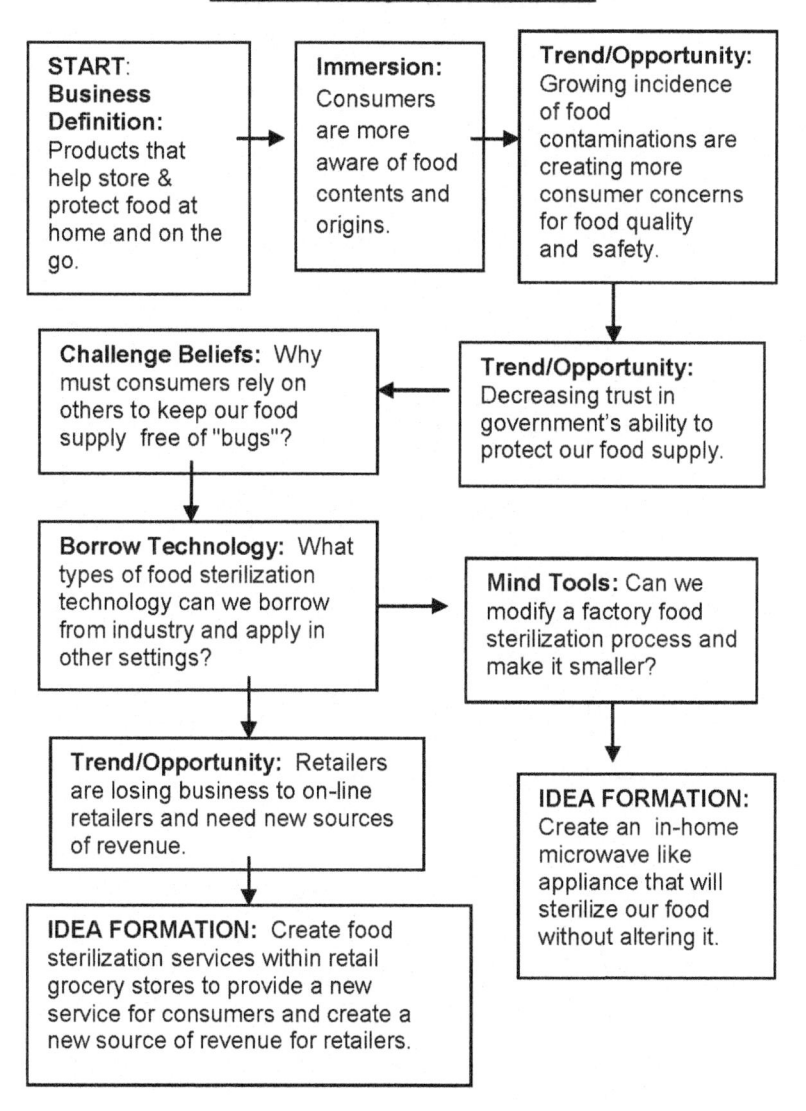

◂ SEARCHING OUTSIDE THE WHITE BOX FOR NEW PRODUCT INNOVATION

IDEA MAPPING (Food Storage 2)
Food Storage & Protection

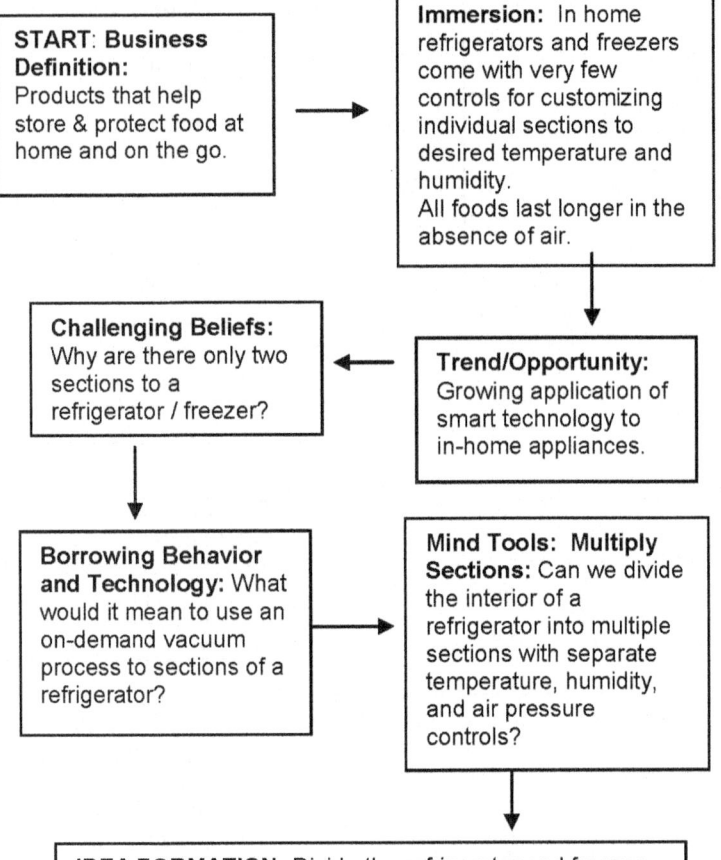

START: Business Definition: Products that help store & protect food at home and on the go.

Immersion: In home refrigerators and freezers come with very few controls for customizing individual sections to desired temperature and humidity.
All foods last longer in the absence of air.

Challenging Beliefs: Why are there only two sections to a refrigerator / freezer?

Trend/Opportunity: Growing application of smart technology to in-home appliances.

Borrowing Behavior and Technology: What would it mean to use an on-demand vacuum process to sections of a refrigerator?

Mind Tools: Multiply Sections: Can we divide the interior of a refrigerator into multiple sections with separate temperature, humidity, and air pressure controls?

IDEA FORMATION: Divide the refrigerator and freezer into multiple sections, customized by the user, in size, temperature, humidity, and air vacuum pressure level to help increase the food storage shelf life for each type of food for its optimal individual storage condition.

VISION DRIVING APPLICATIONS - FOOD STORAGE & PROTECTION

IDEA MAPPING (Food Storage 3)
Food Storage & Protection

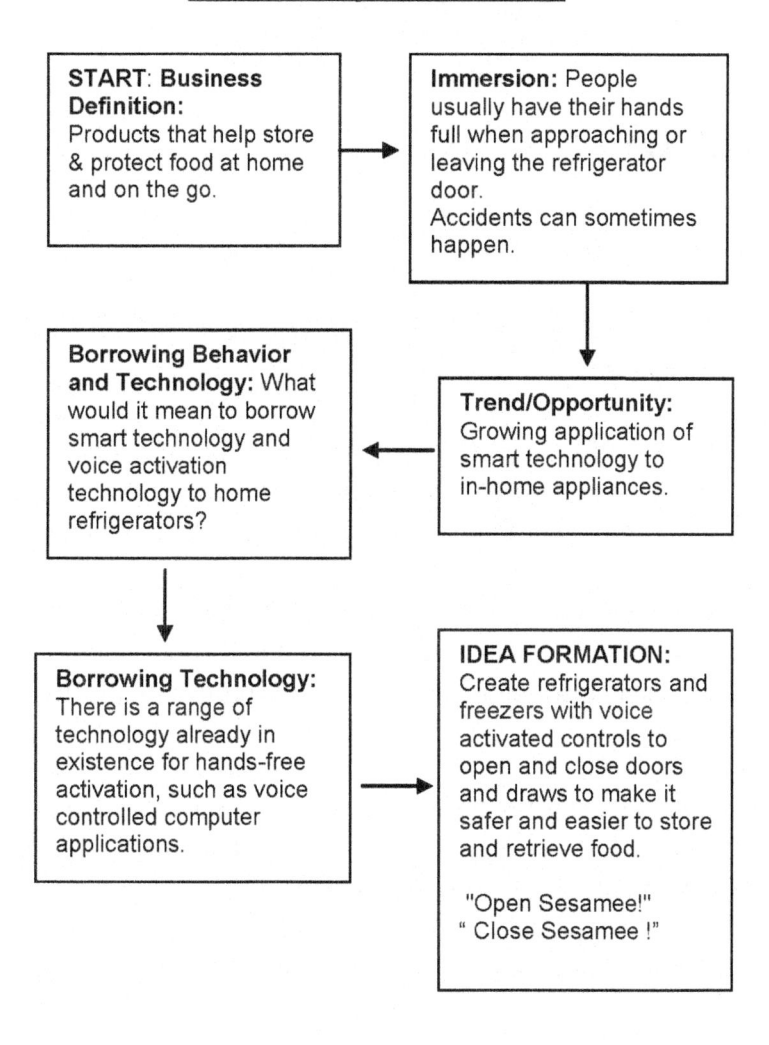

START: Business Definition: Products that help store & protect food at home and on the go.

Immersion: People usually have their hands full when approaching or leaving the refrigerator door. Accidents can sometimes happen.

Trend/Opportunity: Growing application of smart technology to in-home appliances.

Borrowing Behavior and Technology: What would it mean to borrow smart technology and voice activation technology to home refrigerators?

Borrowing Technology: There is a range of technology already in existence for hands-free activation, such as voice controlled computer applications.

IDEA FORMATION: Create refrigerators and freezers with voice activated controls to open and close doors and draws to make it safer and easier to store and retrieve food.

"Open Sesamee!"
" Close Sesamee !"

Summary

This book is founded on my two beliefs regarding key shortcomings in NPD programs:

1. Many NPD programs lack proper management of the fuzzy front end of the NPD idea funnel, by not developing a healthy range of new product ideas, in both quantity and quality.

2. The current best practice approach to NPD ideation as based on fulfilling consumer need-gap White Box opportunities will not likely inspire the generation of disruptive innovative NPD ideas.

More importantly, this book is also founded on my belief that there is a way to address these shortcomings with an NPD ideation process that I call Vision Driving, a process that can build a higher caliber of new ideas in both quality and quantity for any business.

A company's NPD launch success rate can in some way be traced back to the quality of their NPD ideation process, and what they place into their NPD idea funnel. I won't go so far as to suggest that the oft quoted computer science philosophy of "Garbage in, Garbage Out" (GIGO) is applicable here, but there is a relationship. As I fully explain throughout this book, a successful NPD function needs a healthy range of ideas to ensure that the Stage-Gate vetting process

SUMMARY

will provide the company with good ideas, and the right ideas to launch.

Developing new product ideas is a difficult task, and developing disruptive new product ideas is even more challenging. But as we see from history, it is the disruptive new products that have helped advance mankind and businesses in what we call progress. It is also responsible for driving great advances in market position and revenue for those individuals and companies who are able to execute successful disruptive NPD launches.

The Vision Driving process is meant to help. It advances on the need-gap, White Box method of generating NPD ideas, with a series of stimuli that are intended to reveal ideas that are not restrained by any such consumer research. There is a place in competitive strategies where the launch of a disruptive NPD entry is appropriate and possibly necessary. This is where Vision Driving can make a meaningful contribution to the company's objectives. Vision Driving creates disruption.

I am hopeful that you will find this book and its Vision Driving guide to be valuable tools in helping you stay ahead of the competition.

About the Author

Mark William Zabrowsky is Principal in Z-Mark Concepts, Inc, a new product innovation and marketing consultancy. Prior to forming his consulting business, Zabrowsky had a 30 year career in classical consumer packaged goods (CPG) marketing management, new product development (NPD), and strategic planning, in a range of positions within the corporate environment, as a small business consultant, and as an adjunct college professor.

In that time he had developed and launched a wide range of new products in OTC Drugs, consumer medical devices, sports medicine, small appliances, office desk accessories, and household cleaning products. He is credited with several patents, and has written the curriculum book for the college course he taught: *"How to Convert New Product Ideas into Profitable Ventures"*

During his career, Zabrowsky has benefited from working with and learning from some great marketing minds, including Frank Ginsberg, CEO AFG Advertising, Danny Abraham, founder and former CEO of

ABOUT THE AUTHOR

Thompson Medical Company, Ralph Larsen, former CEO of Johnson and Johnson, Peter Mann, founder and former CEO of Prestige Brands Holdings, and Steven Frankel former President of Becton Dickinson Consumer Products.

Zabrowsky has a BME in Mechanical Engineering, MBA in Marketing, and advanced studies in Industrial Design. He has benefited from this diverse set of insights by approaching new products from multiple perspectives at the same time, not as a marketer, not as an R&D guy, not as a designer, and not as a consumer, but as a holistic ideator. His vision goes beyond the traditional linear need-gap approach in uncovering new product ideas. His belief is that there are no small brands, just small brand ideas, and any brand can find the big idea.

Zabrowsky now lives and works in Northern New Jersey.

He can be contacted at Zmarkconceptsinc@gmail.com.